Praise for *Letting Go of the Work You Love*

"This book is a vital and long-overdue contribution to the field of psychotherapy. Too often, therapists exit the profession without a clear plan or intentional closure. This groundbreaking work initiates an essential conversation about how we can end our practices with integrity, clarity, and care. It's not just recommended reading—it's required."

—Joe Kort, PhD, LMSW, author of *Gay Affirmative Therapy for the Straight Clinician* and *Ten Smart Things Gay Men Can Do to Improve Their Lives*

"Unlike traditional jobs, a therapy private practice offers no clear path to retirement. We plan for our clients and careers, but not our own endings. This book fills that gap—helping therapists retire with intention, honoring their meaningful work while preparing for what's next. With prompts, tools, and wise guidance, it addresses the grief, identity shifts, and reflection that come with letting go. As a practice owner, the idea of closing my practice felt overwhelming. This workbook gave me the tools, clarity, language, and peace to do it with integrity. Written by therapists who understand, it helped me—and it will help you too."

—LaNail Plummer, EdD, LPC, author of *The Essential Guide for Counseling Black Women* and Counseling Department chair, Trinity Washington University

"This beautifully written book is so timely for many of us in the healing professions. While it's uncomfortable to consider stopping the work I truly love, this book helps by shining a light on the path ahead. Filled with inherent wisdom, healers of all ages should read this to reframe their outlook and plan for the future."

—Melisa Pearce, LCSW, author of *Touched by a Horse* and contributor for *Horse as Teacher: The Path to Authenticity*

"*Letting Go of the Work You Love* is exactly the book I've needed as I look toward retirement and begin the process of scaling back my caseload. Grodzki and Wehrenberg offer insights and practical tools to prepare for the emotional, financial, legal, and ethical steps involved. A highly recommended resource for any therapist approaching the stage where retirement is becoming a real consideration."

—Linda Hershman, LMFT, author of *Gray Divorce: Everything You Need to Know About Later-Life Breakups*

"Those of us in the helping professions seem to find it extremely challenging to begin contemplating the prospect of retiring. Written with compassion, hope, and practicality, Grodzki and Wehrenberg provide us with a roadmap for navigating both the internal and external realities of this major milestone. No matter where you are in the personal inquiry of retirement, you will find peace of mind in these pages."

—Jennifer G. Anderson, MCC, author of *Plant Yourself Where You Will Bloom*

"As a physician, I loved reading, and I highly recommend *Letting Go of the Work You Love.* It is relevant for any healthcare provider, not only therapists. It provides practical perspective, insights, and information regarding the issue of retirement that I've not seen anywhere else! The book offers a much-needed practical approach for addressing the major questions, emotions, motivations, concerns, and often sensitive issues we are confronted with during the major life-changing transition to retirement. It brought me great peace of mind!"

—Lila McConnell, MD, geriatrician

"This insightful and compassionate book is a must-read for any professional—therapist, coach, or healing professional—contemplating retirement. Their comprehensive four-stage Readiness for Retirement Model is a true gem, offering clarity, emotional support, and practical guidance for navigating one of life's most profound transitions."

—Chrissy Carew, MCC, author of *Insightful Player: Football Pros Lead a Bold Movement of Hope*

Letting Go of the Work You Love

A Workbook for Therapists to Prepare for Retirement, Close a Practice, and End a Career with Integrity

Lynn Grodzki, LCSW, MCC, and
Margaret Wehrenberg, PsyD

LETTING GO OF THE WORK YOU LOVE

Published by
PESI Publishing, Inc.
3839 White Ave
Eau Claire, WI 54703

Cover design by Michelle Lee Lagerroos
Interior design by Emily Dyer
Editing by Abbie Phelps

ISBN 9781683738350 (print)
ISBN 9781683738367 (ePUB)
ISBN 9781683738374 (ePDF)

Printed in the United States of America.

PESI Publishing
pesipublishing.com

Table of Contents

Introduction: A Profession That's Hard to Leave

Jenna, a clinical social worker in private practice, was sixty-five—the average age of those who retire in the United States. Nevertheless, she found herself inwardly cringing every time her husband raised the dreaded topic of retirement.

Her husband, happily retired from his own career, made a good case for the things they might do if she was no longer working: sell the family house and downsize to a condo, spend more time with their grandchildren, and travel more before they were too old. "After working for forty years, aren't you ready for the next phase of life?" he asked. "Isn't it time to take care of yourself instead of caring so much for others?"

"I love what I do," Jenna explained to her peer-supervision group. "I've spent so many years refining my craft. I have a good-sized caseload, and many of my clients would be distraught if I left. My sessions are always interesting. I love the support and friendship I get from this supervision group. I built my practice, and I'm proud of it. I'm not ready to close the door on all this."

It's the uniqueness of our career that makes it challenging, compelling, fulfilling, and exhausting—and ultimately harder to let go of. So how do therapists age out of their profession? And why would they ever leave voluntarily when their work provides so much fulfillment, both personally and professionally? Is there a way to make the topic of retirement easier to discuss for those in their seventies, eighties, or yes, even nineties, before illness or other circumstances force the conversation?

Our Workbook, Our Selves

We (Lynn and Margaret) are therapists, authors, and presenters in our seventies, whose friendship has spanned fifteen years. About five years ago, thoughts about retirement began creeping into our conversations. We wondered whether burnout was causing us to think this way, or if it was a signal that we needed to attend to something related to our changing life stages. One of us (Margaret) made the leap into retirement after taking a few years to wind down with clients (we use this term rather than *patients* throughout this book). The other (Lynn) has chosen not to seek new therapy clients, allowing her caseload to shrink slightly, but hasn't closed her practice. She is still working as a business coach with therapists in private practice, although she's now thinking more seriously about retirement. When we began to research the issue of therapists retiring, we were surprised at the dearth of material on the topic, save for a few journal articles. We decided to dig deeper.

In 2022, we emailed surveys to more than 50 retired or retiring licensed therapists to hear what was difficult for them about the process, what was going well, and above all, how they were handling emotional and psychological issues related to the shift away from their professional identity. Who had they been before retirement? Who were they now? We then conducted follow-up interviews, picking up on common themes related to their deep attachment to clients and the challenges of overidentifying with the therapist role. We reviewed the literature and attended lectures and conferences about retirement. Then we started to write together about retirement and the changing psychotherapy field, and teach. We have now met with more than six hundred therapists through our surveys, workshops, and follow-up interviews to further our understanding of the themes in this book. Our findings and a variety of stories from those we surveyed and interviewed will be included throughout. All examples, anecdotes, and people we have quoted in this book come from our surveys and interviews and are composites with names changed to protect their privacy and identity.

We understand the deep connections many respondents have formed with their professional roles, degrees, licenses, and the training that often becomes central to one's self-identity. We also recognize, as some have shared, how easy it is to become the repository of clients' histories, narratives, hopes, traumas, and dreams—elements that stay with us even after therapy ends. This emotional residue is part of what makes stepping away from the work of being a therapist so challenging. Indeed, many respondents noted that even after they were "officially" retired, they continued to work pro bono, as caring for others was, in many ways, a fundamental part of who they were.

Our professional identities as therapists are often deeply intertwined with our personal lives. Many of those we spoke with identified so strongly with their professional role that when asked how they described or introduced themselves, they prioritized their professional title (e.g., psychotherapist, psychologist, counselor, social worker, clinician) over other roles, such as spouse, parent, partner, or volunteer. They explained that much of their professional work reflected who they were personally—authentic, warm, curious, observant, approachable, and analytical—and that these values and qualities were key to their clinical success.

Respondents also wrote about how being sympathetic and helpful to others as part of their daily work gave them positive feelings. Several even spoke about the addictiveness of the good feeling that helping provides and the way it can interfere with retirement. From this perspective, continuing in the role of therapist can be understood as a compassion or empathy addiction. As with any addiction, to live without it, we need a plan to discover other interests that will nourish us in its place. We don't have to stop being compassionate when we leave our role, but we do need to find new outlets for our desire to help—and perhaps show *ourselves* the same compassion and empathy we show our clients.

Our Businesses Count Too

It's not just the feel-good aspect of our work that keeps us from retiring. Although therapists work in a number of settings, agencies, educational institutions, and medical facilities, many are self-employed, and their businesses literally carry their names. We *are* the businesses we build.

For Mary, who worked in private practice for thirty years, the biggest retirement challenge wasn't letting go of her caseload but letting go of her business. "I was the first woman in my family to be self-supporting," she explained. "I worked hard to build a reputation as a Black therapist. I grew up with a picture of Mary McLeod Bethune on my wall. I was determined to build a brick-and-mortar practice. I bought office space, learned how to network and advertise, hired associates, and handled payroll. This business is my baby!"

Few professions allow people to set up a business so quickly, without a bank loan or even a business plan, and operate it profitably for decades—yet 60 percent of all therapists do just that. These businesses provide clinical autonomy and financial independence, and furthermore, they become a major source of personal pride. This is just another layer of attachment that can be wrenching to dissolve. It's rare and difficult to sell a small private practice, as the main asset is the therapist running it, and her results and reputation aren't easily transferable. Often when therapists retire, they have little choice other than to simply remove their shingle from the wall, close the doors on decades of effort, and say goodbye to clients.

Losing one beloved client can feel like a huge loss, but what about losing your entire caseload? Your practice? Your business? Your professional identity? All this needs to be grieved and processed. It's one reason that taking your time when planning retirement is so important, as is considering your own needs, not just your clients'. Many therapists work in larger areas, such as leadership and management roles or in agencies, clinics, hospitals, nonprofits, or schools. If you are in this situation, retirement may involve letting go of projects, programs, and years of working with a team.

To say it plainly, how do you step away from a valued profession and a fulfilling career with both grace and grit?

Lynn's Story: Self-Reflection

I have been in a process of self-reflection for several years, thinking actively about retirement as well as researching and writing on the topic, but I am not ready to take any formal steps yet. By choice and circumstance (I do a lot of family caregiving), my caseload has been growing smaller each year, but at seventy-four, I'm still happy to have it.

Warren Buffett says he values time more than money, but he wants to work for as long as he can because he enjoys running his business. Today, in good health and with plenty of energy, I feel the same way—many therapists in my position likely do as well. A part of my hesitation about retirement is that I haven't yet defined what it could offer me that's better than the satisfaction and purpose I find in my work right now.

During my early years of coaching training, I often heard the phrase "I'm in the question of . . ." This fits where I am now. It validates my need to stay in a place of not knowing, and the richness of allowing a big question to unfold. For me, being in the question of retirement is like walking through a verdant forest full of unknown paths and interesting things to ponder. What would I do with more time? What's missing from my life that retirement might offer? What could I do that would match the connection and fulfillment of this work?

When asked if I'm going to retire, I like to say I'm engaged in the question—which gives me a reason to keep asking others about their experience, listening to my own emotional responses, wondering and pondering without pressure, and experimenting with new activities, all to explore what my own retirement might look like.

I know that retirement is often a time of ambiguity, but it doesn't distress me. I've slowed down but haven't yet received a clear signal to stop. You might say I'm waiting. For someone who's been proactive throughout their career, waiting can be uncomfortable, but I'm cultivating patience and learning to appreciate the mystery of whatever comes next. I'm allowing my life and my work to evolve organically, in their own ways.

Margaret's Story: Moving Forward

I often get asked by other therapists how I could've stopped working in the midst of a flourishing career. "Why stop doing what you're good at?" they'd wonder. One colleague has questioned me about this repeatedly, as if by deciding to retire I'm letting someone down. The truth is, I made the decision after the joy I'd long found in the work had begun to diminish, and I was feeling increasingly fatigued. What these colleagues haven't considered is that, regardless of the fulfillment we may get from facilitating therapy, it's still work and can become depleting.

Many therapists who answered our survey described what I felt after five decades in the mental health field: the weight of responsibility. Caring for my clients, being available and on time every week, and learning and utilizing the most up-to-date methods—it all began to feel heavy. I knew this awareness would interfere with being fully engaged in each and every session. I wanted more time for self-care and for my life outside the office.

After decades of loving my work, I still wanted to be helpful, but I could use my empathy and compassion in a less demanding way, volunteering at a job where I could skip a week or a month without abandoning or hurting anyone.

The realization that it was time to retire, abrupt as it was, caused me to rapidly contemplate what the consequences of retirement were for my clients. I needed to give them time to prepare. I learned that consideration of each client's needs, giving them substantial notice and time to reflect on our relationship and their own lives, was the first step to a successful retirement.

Now that I am retired, I feel lighter, more cheerful, and more energetic. The first several months of retirement challenged me to adjust my lifestyle and weekly schedule. This was disconcerting at first—my "normal" pace of life had shifted dramatically. But now, I'm reaping the benefits of my newfound flexibility, which includes enjoying freedom to write without pressure.

How to Use This Workbook

What does it take not just to retire, but to retire *well*? We think readiness may be the key. Having a process to think and plan for retirement starts long before we give clients notice.

Time is your friend in retirement planning. You may need months or years to lay the groundwork. For example, a year ahead of your retirement date, you may start screening which clients and diagnoses are appropriate for you to see, given your retirement deadline. You have to be sensitive to client needs when giving them notice so they can have sufficient time to end well—reviewing what brought them to therapy, how they feel about you and their relationship with you, and what the loss of this relationship may mean for them.

It's important to note that therapists aren't without feelings in this process. It's a challenge to end the therapy relationship and not allow our own feelings to interfere, so take careful note of reactivity that might surface, and give yourself time to process your own feelings first.

Maintaining boundaries around a retirement plan is as important as maintaining boundaries during the normal process of therapy. Without a plan, retiring can feel like quitting. It can feel like we're deserting our clients and prioritizing ourselves over those who need us. Leaving with guilt or regret, or judging ourselves as uncompassionate, won't help us create a vibrant life after practice. Leaping into retirement with no plan is like swinging on a trapeze with no safety net. Preparing to retire well must include a recommitment to what you genuinely love to do.

So, where are you on your retirement journey? Without a clear framework for the stages of change in retirement, even those approaching retirement may find the process of closing a clinical career daunting and uncertain. The Readiness for Retirement Model, which outlines four essential stages, I) precontemplation, II) contemplation, III) preparation, and IV) action, will help you navigate this transition with greater confidence and clarity.

Stage I, precontemplation, will address all the worries, feelings, and doubts that can create obstacles to fully accepting and welcoming the idea of retirement. You will learn how to negotiate the internal struggles that may be affecting your deliberation and take a careful look at the many options for ending a career. Over time, the combination of working and helping can become a powerful compulsion that is hard to let go. Therefore, we will explore how you can transform your mindset. You will learn how to separate and claim your personal sense of skills, talents, and self-worth that are distinct from your professional achievement.

Endings in therapy are often complex, but those initiated by the therapist for retirement require special consideration. Stage II of the model will prepare you—and your clients—to be grounded and centered to weather the potential disruption that your retirement may cause. You will learn to anticipate the complicated reactions to a therapist-initiated "forced" ending and see recommendations to make the process of ending treatment easier and more collaborative.

In stage III of the Readiness for Retirement Model, you will create a comprehensive retirement plan to help you close your practice safely, ethically, and legally, saying goodbye to the business, administrative, and financial aspects of therapy. You will explore your relationship with money, address any limiting beliefs, and think logically to create a customized retirement budget.

What comes next after retirement? Stage IV of the model will help you to embrace the legacy of your career, define your "retirement identity," and connect with your future self to discover what awaits you beyond the profession.

Whether you are in solo practice or in a leadership role, this workbook can further your steps toward readiness. Begin with the next section, titled "Getting Started: The Readiness for Retirement Model," where we will guide you through the four stages in more detail. Stage by stage, through the successive chapters of this book, you will see the Readiness for Retirement Model unfold. As you progress, we will walk you through the emotions, thoughts, shifts, and actions that are important to stay proactive and positive.

Throughout the book, we encourage you to use a retirement journal for deepening your comprehension and experience. It can be kept in the pages of this workbook, or you can use a separate notebook, computer document, or diary of your choice. We will offer prompts for when to use your journal. As you process and shift, stage by stage, you can ultimately plan a retirement process that works best for you and your clients, practices, or organizations.

After the "Getting Started" section, beginning at chapter 1 will make the most sense, although you can dip into any chapter that sparks your interest. Each chapter has cases, anecdotes, and exercises with ideas and queries to deepen your own critical thinking. This workbook and its Readiness for Retirement Model will support your ability to be aware, thoughtful, prepared, and optimistic as you move forward.

Retirement is more than just ending a career; it's a new beginning. This workbook invites your thinking and planning as you move ahead with your own retirement journey. Use the exercises, checklists, and retirement journal to help you make sense of the many challenges that leaving the profession can bring. Then, take the next steps in crafting a plan that allows you to end your career with completion and compassion.

Are you ready to start? It's time to take the first step and explore the Readiness for Retirement Model.

Getting Started: Readiness for Retirement

This is a book about how, when, and why therapists retire and the many questions, concerns, and feelings that need to be understood, worked through, and resolved in order for you to retire well.

As therapists (and by this term, we mean psychotherapists, psychiatrists, psychologists, social workers, counselors, psychiatric nurses, marriage and family therapists, and other mental health professionals), we have a unique role in health care; our career path, including our process of retirement, is not the same as other health care providers'. To put this in context, in the United States, we have recently seen an exodus in health care, with over three hundred thousand professionals—doctors, nurses, and other related specialists—retiring and leaving the field in just a single year, citing burnout, low pay, high stress, and long hours for their decision (Landi, 2022). They are aging, tired, and ready to stop working.

But in the midst of this mass exit, one branch of the health care profession is not leaving their offices with the same urgency. Therapists are staying put—we generally remain in our clinical seats long beyond those in other health care careers.

What makes us reluctant to retire? It's not that we don't face the same hardships as other professionals. We are also the victims of burnout, low pay, high stress, and long hours. But for a therapist, especially one in private practice, age may just be a number, not a signal that it's time to leave. As one therapist explained, "It takes time to age into this career, and it's equally challenging to age out."

The distinctiveness of our role, the ways that it is unlike other health care providers', may make it ultimately harder to walk away. First and foremost, therapists see their clients (as mentioned earlier, we use this term rather than *patients* throughout this book) more frequently and consistently than any other kind of health care provider. It's not unusual for clients and therapists to meet once or even twice a week for years in ongoing treatment. Talking is a major tool in psychotherapy and counseling, and unlike other health care providers, therapists hear about all aspects of our clients' lives. The attachment that develops with these frequent, confidential, client-focused, open-ended sessions often provides a critical ongoing lifeline for vulnerable clients; this is not an easy bond for any therapist, even one who longs to retire, to sever.

Treatment demands are not the only factors that make it difficult for us to consider retirement. Therapists must always consider ethical codes that require us to not abandon our clients. We have to consider the timing, pacing, options, and notification when leaving our caseloads, a process that can take years to coordinate. We must balance the external demands that may be urging us toward retirement with the internal responsibilities and ties to clients that our work requires. For those of us in leadership or management positions in agencies, clinics, group practices, associations, or organizations, there are additional layers of complexity in the reality of stepping down.

Perhaps the biggest problem in retirement for therapists is that we are often clueless about the topic; before writing this book, the two of us searched the professional literature for guidance about how to end the work of therapy, close a practice, or look ahead to a post-retirement life. There was little to find. Therapists are noted for their dedication to training and refining their methods throughout the arc of their careers. It is striking that so little has been taught or offered to clinicians in the form of a planned and positive exit path.

No wonder we are so uncertain about when, how, or why to leave our work. Without guidance, even for those of retirement age, closing down a career becomes a constantly moving target. As one psychotherapist explains, "At age sixty-five, the closer I think I am to determining my retirement date, the more it keeps advancing into the distance. My friends who are lawyers, teachers, or business owners seem to have it easier, especially in terms of knowing when it is time to stop working and then taking the prescribed steps. But I am always in a position of waiting for direction. I don't know when I will be ready or even how that decision will happen."

The Path to Readiness

How does a therapist get ready to retire? Do you wait for an *Aha* moment, the sudden insight that it's the right time to walk away? Or does the decision happen slowly, over months or years, as you circle around the idea like a pilot trying to land a small plane without practice, inevitably resulting in a bumpy landing? Do you reduce your client list so that you work less each year—until you leave, as T.S. Eliot phrased it, "not with a bang but a whimper?" Do you abruptly decide you are done, set a date, and say goodbye without looking back? Or do you retire with a careful and thoughtful plan?

The path to retirement is complicated. We are bound by our licensure, ethical codes, contractual agreements, attachment to clients, need to find necessary referrals, and legal requirements. Retirement raises questions for a therapist at every stage, in part because retiring is not a solo event. Therapists have many others in their orbit—their clients, colleagues, practices, associates, interns, students, and organizations—who may be deeply affected.

With so little guidance from traditional professional sources, such as courses, peer support groups, or clinical supervision, a therapist's decision to end a practice is often made alone, in isolation. Our research, including surveys and interviews with therapists who were in the process of retiring or had successfully retired, suggests that retirement strategies are varied, often unformed and unplanned, and filled with uncertainty—even after the decision is made.

Leaving a purposeful, meaningful career requires more than simply walking away. We care about the people we will impact and affect in our retirement. We want a way to leave well, using the skills and values that our profession has instilled in us. We need to know why, when, and how to retire. We need a beneficial, reliable roadmap, customized for each of us. Welcome to the Readiness for Retirement Model.

The Readiness for Retirement Model

After thinking about our own situations (Margaret has retired and Lynn is still working) and discussing the topic together for years, we began to research and write. We began informally, then shifted to more formal surveys and interviews of therapists in all stages of retirement. Following these, we wrote an article for the *Psychotherapy Networker* magazine (Grodzki & Wehrenberg, 2024); then, based on reader response, we began to develop and teach retirement workshops.

Not surprisingly, we found confusion and questions about the retirement process in those we talked with and taught. We responded to this by organizing our ideas into a model of change intended specifically for therapists who want to retire well. As we developed this model, we gravitated toward a perspective grounded in behavioral change, one that could enhance readiness. Many of us are familiar with the Transtheoretical Model developed by Prochaska and DiClemente (1983) in the late 1970s, often referred to as the Stages of Change Model; it has six steps to help clients make a lasting, significant change from an unwanted behavior, like alcohol addiction or smoking.

We found that four of these six stages (precontemplation, contemplation, preparation, and action) seemed applicable to how therapists think about, prepare, and plan for their retirement. However, as written in the original model, the four stages were not sufficient to describe the journey of retirement. We needed to develop each stage further to include the many considerations that are unique when leaving a therapy practice. From our research, study, teaching, and interviews with therapists, we began to identify themes and topics, and we then were able to weave a tapestry of ideas and solutions that could connect to the four stages. We started to envision a successful process to guide a therapist's journey through a process of retirement. This is now the basis of our Readiness for Retirement Model.

Our model is more evolution than revolution; it outlines a natural process of change. The stages follow each other in an intuitively progressive manner. Stage by stage, the Readiness for Retirement Model leads therapists on an insightful and deliberate path. We allow for a customized planning process, an important component of a retirement model since therapists work within a variety of situations, practices, and roles. The Readiness for Retirement Model can be especially helpful for therapists because it is so relatable: It speaks our language, using a theoretical concept of change merged with our profession's direct experience.

The process of retirement for therapists is complex. We must address not just the "how to" but the "how to *be*." The psychological and emotional issues that surface during this change are real and need to be understood, worked through, and hopefully resolved—ahead of retirement.

Here is an overview of the four stages of the Readiness for Retirement Model:

I. Precontemplation: The Stay or Go Dilemma

II. Contemplation: The Therapeutic Conversation

III. Preparation: The Logistics of Letting Go

IV. Action: A New Beginning

Each section of this book represents a stage of the model and includes three chapters that explore the challenges, ideas, and solutions involved in preparing for retirement. As you progress through the chapters, you'll discover ways to expand your thinking and emotions, find answers to your questions, and gain the confidence to move forward. The following sections provide a brief overview of each stage to help you reflect on your own situation. As you read, consider responding to the included retirement journaling prompts to deepen your understanding.

I. Precontemplation: The Stay or Go Dilemma

Jonah, who was fifty-five, attended one of our recent workshops on retirement and told the group that he would not consider retiring for at least ten years. "I don't need to think about this now. But it is always helpful to me, in my planning, to hear what is ahead, even if it is way, way down the road," he said. If you, like Jonah, are not near retirement age or have no thoughts of retiring, you are probably in the stage of precontemplation. In this stage, retirement is not an immediate consideration, at least not consciously or outwardly.

However, some therapists are firmly in this stage, not because they are too young to think about retirement, but because they are in denial. They just don't want to think about ever leaving their work. There are many valid reasons to not think about retirement: You might be happy working, in good health, and planning to continue indefinitely. You might be close to retirement age after coming into the profession late and still want to work, learn, and practice more. You might feel like you just got here and have no desire to stop, even if your peers are leaving.

Some say that retirement is not an option for them; it's a financial luxury they can't entertain. For these therapists, staying in precontemplation instead of planning may feel more practical. Why think about something you will never have?

Rosa, a counselor in a rural area mental health clinic, admitted that she would love to retire and was of an age to do so, but she and her extended family needed the income from her job. "I am glad I have some control over my hours and my schedule, but the retirement conversation is off the table as long as my grandkids are living with us and need my income."

Staying in the stage of precontemplation can become problematic when a therapist who needs to make a change—or at least consider the implications of retirement based on health, psychological capacity, or various situational reasons—still denies that any retirement planning is necessary. For some of us, precontemplation can signal a blind spot; we are not irreplaceable or immortal. Unfortunately, it's hard to see past some of our gaps. In our profession, many of us are aging, and we practice without measures in place to monitor our capacity and ability, let alone sufficient feedback to know if we need to think seriously about letting go.

Allan, an analyst in his early nineties, had been much revered in his community but was now often physically impaired. He had issues of falling asleep during therapy sessions, to the distress of his clients and the colleagues with whom he shared an office. He adamantly refused to discuss his problems or his declining health. He had no plan for retiring, no money saved, and not even a thought of how or when to alert clients that would need necessary referrals. He stayed mired in a heightened sense of inflated self, saying that "even my bad days are better than most others' good days."

Sometimes we stay in precontemplation due to a sense of futility: We have tried to leave before without success, so we stay and stay.

Natalie insisted that she had "tried hard" to leave her busy agency role as an addiction counselor several times before. She admitted she was in poor health, but each time she had approached her supervisor with an end date, she had been talked into delaying her retirement. Her supervisor had told her there was no one to take over her position and that the overwhelming number of clients flooding the agency needed her services. Now, for reasons of guilt as well as a basic reluctance to begin the complicated process of change, she said that she would simply stay "until they have to carry me out in a stretcher."

To shift from precontemplation and consider a change, focus on providing reasons why such a change can be positive. Consider what will happen if *no* change occurs. What does the extended future look like? If you are stuck in precontemplation about retirement, even when others close to you have told you that they are concerned for your health or well-being, the chapters in this first section will be constructive and beneficial.

RETIREMENT JOURNAL

Reflecting on Precontemplation

If you worry that retirement is necessary but you struggle with some internal denial, reflect on the following prompts in your retirement journal:

- Why is it difficult for you to even think about retirement?
- What gets in your way of considering this as a positive idea?
- What feelings do you experience that stop you from thinking or planning?
- How long can you continue working at this same pace?
- Is there a threat to your physical or mental health or well-being based on this degree of work?
- What do others say to you about your need to retire? In what ways do you agree and disagree with their opinions?
- What measures or feedback do you use to assess your degree of competence or effectiveness in your work?
- Who can you talk to about retirement safely and securely, without feeling pressured?

II. Contemplation: The Therapeutic Conversation

To contemplate means to carefully observe, think, meditate, and reflect. For therapists, this second stage of the Readiness for Retirement Model is more complex than it may be for most other professions. We are lifelines for many, and leaving those vulnerable people in the midst of treatment is not something we can do quickly or impulsively. We are often not easily replaceable in our roles. Once we have moved through precontemplation and can accept and welcome that retirement is going to take place, we next have to think of each and every relationship that our leaving will affect: our clients and colleagues; our commitments to those in our clinics, group practices, educational institutions, or agencies; and our students or supervisees. These relationships form the basis of treatment, programs, and outreach and need careful consideration to bring to an end.

Contemplation means reflecting on our clinical philosophy and methodology and how those will inform our process of letting go. The outcome of the contemplative stage is to have a clearer idea of who will be impacted by our leaving, what to anticipate in ending treatment, and how we need to prepare to say goodbye to those who depend on us for their mental health.

Like the first stage of the model, contemplation takes time to shift through. Just as you do your own process work, you need to first address your own emotional issues, beliefs, and concerns that may get triggered when you end your cases. Then you will need to do a deep dive into thinking about your clinical caseload to anticipate what your clients will need to end well.

Some therapists find it hard to retire because of the responsibility of their caseload or due to the projects or teams they lead.

Talia was eighty years old and owned a group practice in the Northeast; although she had reduced her own client caseload, she still felt very attached to the practice. She had delegated administration to an office manager and hired associates to see clients, but she still worked as the clinical director. She had talked about selling or closing down the practice for several years, but had not yet taken any steps. She complained about the stress of owning the practice and said repeatedly that she needed to retire for her "health and sanity" but still could not take a step forward. Her family got tired of hearing the same litany of complaints, as Talia revisited the topic of retirement in almost every conversation, with anyone who would listen. Ultimately, she was unable to decide which was better: to stay or go.

Finally, her grown daughter, tired of the seemingly endless conversation, made an unusual request. She asked Talia to accompany her at a seven-day silent Buddhist retreat. For a week, Talia sat with her own thoughts. She could not talk about them to dispel her anxiety or repeat her pro and con lists out loud, and found herself sad and grieving. At the end of the week, however, after tears and long meditations, Talia had moved forward a step. "I need to do some therapy to understand my grief and reluctance. I am going to stop talking about this outside of therapy. Until then, I will stop complaining and just try to explore my ambivalence so I can move ahead with a decision."

Albert Einstein is frequently attributed with having said, "You cannot solve a problem with the same mind that created it." It helps to understand the nature of your own ambivalence and to shift your way of thinking, to find a different perspective to lead you out of it. For Talia, a silent retreat helped her to shift to a different viewpoint, enough to see a pattern about ambivalence itself.

If you find it difficult to imagine leaving your clients or teams and feel worried, anxious, or stuck in contemplation about retirement, the chapters in this second section will be especially valuable. You'll gain a deeper understanding of why endings in therapy can be challenging and learn strategies for addressing client attachment and countertransference when a therapist retires. Additionally, you'll explore your own experiences and emotions surrounding endings, as well as any personal beliefs or attachment patterns that might make transitioning away from your caseload or work more difficult.

RETIREMENT JOURNAL

Reflecting on Contemplation

If your thinking feels stuck in a loop, your decision-making process is unproductive, or your pro-and-con list keeps repeating without resolution, take a moment to reflect on the following prompts in your retirement journal:

- What goals and values that you hold dear are in conflict regarding retirement?
- Note your emotional reactions, including longing, fear, guilt, excitement, worry, and other feelings, that surface as you think about planning a retirement date.
- What feels safe about *not* making a decision?
- What issues seem impossible to resolve? Where are you blocked and unable to formulate a way to move forward? What worries feel the most difficult to address?
- List any benefits your retirement might provide for you and for others.
- What kind of support do you currently have in terms of colleagues, peers, or close family and friends that help to keep you on track? If you are lacking in this support, where can you find the resources you need?

III. Preparation: The Logistics of Letting Go

Maya was ready to retire based on her own health issues and a need to do some caregiving for her husband, but she had many questions about how to take the right steps. "I am tired and would leave work tomorrow, but I have so many things to figure out. How do I tell clients I am leaving and when? What do I do if I can't find referrals, since so many of my clients are Medicaid and few therapists in my area are providers? Should I keep my license or let it lapse? Are there legal and ethical issues

I need to be aware of? It's overwhelming and probably why I have been dragging my heels for the past few years. I am eager to retire, but I don't know the actual steps."

In the third stage of the Ready for Retirement Model, preparation, you need pragmatic information that answers the question of *What do I do next?*

In this stage, you will see chapters outlining how to get ready, be organized, and start to experiment with making changes, starting small and becoming larger and larger. Whether you are going to close a solo practice or exit from an expansive leadership role, you will learn to set realistic goals and develop a timeline for change.

We offer you a ten-step retirement plan that covers all the essential practical information and actions for ending a practice with confidence and care. We provide an understanding of how to shift your attention to the additional nonclinical tasks within the scope of business ownership, leadership, or directing a team, to end all aspects of your career with a sense of completion.

This preparation stage is critical before moving onto the final action stage because it allows you to feel secure about the many pragmatic action steps that you need to accomplish.

RETIREMENT JOURNAL

Reflecting on Preparation

If you are ready and willing to start making changes toward retirement, reflect on the following prompts in your retirement journal:

- What information are you missing to feel secure and ready to retire?
- How can you feel safe and secure in your planning?
- Who do you need to talk to and what do you need to research to add to your planning?
- Where do you feel optimistic and ready in your planning process? Where do you feel anxious and worried?
- What can increase your resolve for this stage?
- In the past, how have you found the strength to overcome obstacles? What aspects of that strength can you bring to this planning process?
- What is your vision of a good retirement at this point in the process?

IV. Action: A New Beginning

Paula retired after thirty years in practice as a counselor. She had worked in an agency, taught at a local college as adjunct faculty, and then signed on as an independent contractor in a group private practice. She had a busy career and felt ready to retire. She was surprised at the emotional aftermath, the loss and sadness that lingered for the next year.

"I did everything right to end my career, but I wasn't prepared for the level of grief I still feel about leaving," she said. "I think I missed a step in my retirement planning because I literally feel empty. I was so focused on the logistics and all the arrangements of ending—resigning from insurance panels, sending notification to clients, transferring people to other providers, filling out the application to turn in my licensure, and ending things in the right way—that I didn't think much about what I would need for myself. I literally feel empty and lost in retirement. This was supposed to be what I had waited for. What can I do?"

We interviewed therapists who expressed a sense of optimism and adventure once they could be "all in" with their retirement plans by embracing this fourth and final stage of the Readiness to Retire Model. Optimism is highly correlated with this final stage of readiness since behavioral change studies suggest that when we are filled with pessimism, we focus only on problems and obstacles. Optimists, on the other hand, recognize opportunities and possibilities (Greer, 2023).

The Readiness for Retirement Model is not only about the process of walking away from your career; it's also about knowing what you are walking toward. Part of a good plan is understanding what you take with you, in terms of your legacy, and how it will serve you in the future. In this final stage, we help you see your accomplishments and your legacy, which most therapists tend to underestimate. Knowing all that you have done and the ripple effect of your work can help you be more willing to let go with satisfaction. We also look at the identity that you may adopt in your retirement, which can open new doors and opportunity. Finally, we help you envision your future with a sense of potentiality and engagement.

The chapters in this stage can be a springboard for more excitement and optimism about your future.

RETIREMENT JOURNAL

Reflecting on Action

When thinking about life after retirement, reflect on the following prompts in your retirement journal:

- How have you adjusted to major changes in life in the past? What helps you stay flexible and tolerant of change?
- What are you hoping that a well-planned retirement will bring for you and for others around you?
- What is an example of your resolve that has helped you move forward in life or work?
- What next steps can you take to secure a good retirement plan that would be easy for you?
- How can your resilience drive your readiness for retirement?

Moving Forward

Now that you understand more about your situation within the basic flow of the four stages of our Readiness for Retirement Model, we will begin to examine each of the stages in more detail, beginning with Stage I: Precontemplation: The Stay or Go Dilemma.

Remember, change is difficult. According to Prochaska and Prochaska (1999), we often resist accepting the need for change for several common reasons: we feel we can't, don't want to, don't know how to, or aren't sure what needs to change. Embedded within each of these obstacles is a kernel of resistance—and for therapists facing retirement, this resistance can be especially intricate and challenging to navigate.

To overcome these challenges, readiness is essential. It is best understood as a state of mind—one that fosters clarity, confidence, and resilience. Our Readiness for Retirement Model is designed to support you through each step, helping you feel calmer, more informed, and better prepared for what lies ahead. Readiness provides the trust needed to transition from one stage to the next. No matter where you are on your retirement journey, increasing your readiness can help you feel more secure and optimistic about the road ahead.

Stage I

Precontemplation: The Stay or Go Dilemma

In the *precontemplation* stage of the Readiness for Retirement Model, you may be thinking about retirement, but not in a serious or constructive way. Your thoughts may be filled with ambivalence, and with so much uncertainty, the idea of retiring might feel premature. You may also feel pushed toward a decision by those around you or pulled by circumstances beyond your control.

At this stage, retirement may seem to generate more questions than answers. The perceived negatives outweigh the positives, making it difficult to fully consider the transition. Even if you are at retirement age, you may find it uncomfortable to linger on the thought of eventually stepping away from your work.

In the three chapters that compose this stage, see how to better understand the obstacles that cloud your thinking. Explore any underlying confusion and clarify your goals. Take the time to work through your thoughts and feelings to allow the advantages and benefits of a retirement plan to emerge.

— Chapter 1 —

Push and Pull Factors

At age sixty-eight, I (Margaret) was driving to my office one morning and was hit with a realization: *I do not want to do this.*

It was not just a momentary desire for a day off. It was the first time I experienced a strong feeling of no longer wanting to do the work of my career. At that time, I had been working in the field of mental health for forty-seven years, since the week I turned twenty-one. Then, I was a new college grad and in need of a job. I found one at a Pritzker Children's Hospital, a residential psychiatric facility for children in Chicago. I found my career when I found that job. Over the various iterations of my career, I had never tired of the work with clients—until that day in the car.

I imagined that when I finally retired, it would be because something new grabbed my interest, or I was pulled to do a new activity. I knew I would retire soon-ish; to use the language of readiness for change, I had moved from precontemplation early in my sixties to actively contemplating when would be the right time. Yet, this sudden recognition surprised me: I was tired of the work. We all know what it is to feel tired because of hard work—exhausted by working long days, emotionally drained from dealing with a crisis, or exasperated with too many weeks without a break. We need a day off, or a vacation! This was different, a wake-up call that I no longer wanted to work in this *career*. For the first time, I felt tired *of* the work. I knew I had to make decisions about retirement—and fast.

This distinction between tired *because of working* and tired *of the work* is an important distinction to assess readiness for retiring. Being tired of the work is a classic push factor for people who have the luxury of a choice: retire now or retire at a later time. It is not the only push factor, nor is it a necessary one, but being tired *of the work* suggested to me that it was time to seriously contemplate how to get ready for retirement.

Contemplation and preparation are likely to take some time because therapists have so many considerations about their type of clientele and their business situation. In fact, those stages might overlap a bit. For example, as a solo practitioner, my preparation began when I was still contemplating a serious retirement date. I had envisioned retiring around the age of seventy, and I had set things up, like my finances and business details, with that end date in mind. But in my early sixties, I stopped accepting any new client with a serious trauma history. If I was to retire in five years or less, I could not promise availability for the duration of therapy that a person with trauma might need. Then, in my midsixties, I began to only accept clients with straightforward anxiety problems, referring onward any prospective client who might have a personality disorder or multiple complex mental health concerns. Those client decisions, even without a specific retirement date, turned out to be wise. My remaining caseload could be completed or referred onward.

However, I was missing something. I had spent little time contemplating what I wanted to retire *from*, and almost no time specifically thinking about what I was retiring *to*. What was pulling me toward a life beyond my career? While push factors might be the most powerful reasons why you *need* to retire, pull factors make it clear why you *want* to retire. These details can help determine how the process will unfold.

Push Factors

There are so many reasons to let go of your career. Life can sometimes make it abruptly clear; these are the *push factors*: the things in life that nudge—or outright shove—you away from your career.

In the most immediate way, you can be pushed into retirement when the agency you work for makes it nonnegotiable. Employers can simply end your career because of your age or their economic situation. This can happen working for a university, a hospital, or a community organization, as money and arbitrary rules are not in our control. An involuntary retirement can be completely unexpected; if you do not retire by choice, it will have an impact on how you begin this phase of life.

Other push factors usually happen more gradually. You may notice one day that things are "not how they used to be"—regarding yourself, your clients, or in the world in general. Though change is a necessary part of life and a therapy career in general, these changes can be signs that retirement may be something to consider.

Aging

If you work as a solo practitioner or in a group practice, you have much more power over the timing of your departure, but there are still factors that can push you out, such as declining health. The older you are, the more likely it is that your health has an impact on your career. Chronic illnesses can interfere in so many ways, as occurred to Marjorie, a therapist with a chronic illness whose symptoms waxed and waned, causing too many days out of the office. She realized her unpredictability put a strain on client relationships. Serious illnesses like this can strain your overall energy and cognitive focus, forcing you out of your career earlier than you planned. The list of potential health issues is long.

Many of us over sixty-five feel younger than our age in years and do not focus on the realities of age-related decline. In the U.S. demographic, people over the age of sixty will have about twenty years of life expectancy, but it won't all be in good health. Emotionally, people do not focus on the last five of their remaining years that are likely *not* to be spent in good health. Many psychotherapists tend to believe *I can work as long as I can think.* Because we do not have jobs that require physical vigor, it is easy to meet aging with denial. It is easy to miss the impact of getting tired more easily or feeling aches and pains more regularly. But our clients do notice. They may wonder if they are boring you because you look drowsy. They might act concerned if you seem stiff or have trouble getting out of the easy chair in your office. Perhaps you laugh off these evidences of aging as insignificant to your work ability, yet these moments demonstrate the ways we may be in denial. Health issues can push us out of our career suddenly or gradually, but we should anticipate that our health won't hold forever when we contemplate the timing of leaving our work.

Another infinitely more subtle cause of retirement is mental decline. A certain degree of forgetfulness begins to affect us all as we age. Most of us will develop memory gaffes, mentally looking for the precise word we want even if we have a large supply of substitutes. As much as we might not want it to be true, we may forget names and need to hear details more than once. It may not be a therapeutic issue if we forget the name of a client's sister whom she seldom discusses—but it is a much bigger issue if we forget discussions with that client about a sister who sexually abused her. Some details are important!

Setting aside different problems such as dementia, forgetfulness about significant events and details comes upon most of us slowly, and assessing its significance is hard. We must remain open to recognizing our memory issues and be aware of the difference between occasional forgetfulness and being unable to remember important details of our clients' lives.

Familial Need

It may also be that the health of your loved one becomes a push factor toward your retirement. Many of the professionals who responded to our survey indicated that they were capable of employment, but they needed to care for a spouse or loved one and felt a desire to make the most of the time they had left with this person. It made sense to stop working and start caregiving.

Caring for a family member with a chronic or terminal illness is time-consuming and stressful—in situations like these, the push factor of eliminating the stress that comes with working outside the home makes sense.

I (Lynn) have become a caregiver for my aging father. Caregiving, even with help in place, is a part-time job and required that I reduce my caseload. I still want to continue with the parts of my work that are energizing and important to me, but I'm using my time more intentionally. Taking care of an aging parent puts me in touch with mortality, something that was not my daily focus prior to this caregiving role.

Technology

Other push factors are more within our control. It is easier to be aware of our attitudes to the world around us and the social environment in which our clients are living. As older therapists, we might just not *want* to learn how to navigate new technologies. A 2013 survey showed just 40 percent of adults aged 65–74 used the internet on a daily basis; only 5 percent got most or all of their calls on a cell phone; and just 11 percent sometimes texted (Smith, 2013). The next decade made a lot of difference. As of 2024, nearly everyone has a cell phone, most of which are smartphones, and 75 percent of people over the age of 65 use the internet regularly, though only 8 percent say they are online constantly in the way young adults are (Gelles-Watnick, 2024). It is clear that elders have upped their technology game.

However, being able to text is not the same as being technologically savvy. Staying in the technology game also requires therapists to actively use all types of social media, not just for client connectedness, but also for their own marketing and career development. Even if therapists eschew social media on their own behalf, staying relevant means knowing how social media works and how clients' lives are affected by their engagement with social media.

There is a lot to keep up with, especially if you are not interested enough to use it on your own. Some clients are looking to engage with their therapists on social media, which you may not want to do. You not only need the skills to use different sites and apps, but also must work out how interacting with clients over social media fits your concepts of professionalism and boundaries. Therapists who have been working for many years likely have enough referrals to keep going because of longtime presence in the areas where they work. But if you move to another city, as some do when they are close to retirement or their spouse retires, marketing your practice in a new location necessitates an online presence. This can be a strong push factor toward retirement.

Connection

The expectation that therapy be provided in-person saw an about-face during the pandemic. That period of isolation set the stage for the rapid rise of online psychotherapy options. The idea of developing a real rapport and ongoing relationship is shifting with the advent of therapy provided via phones, sometimes even using avatars so that clients and therapists never see each other's faces.

One of the major online therapy companies advertises that you can change therapists at any time, no questions asked, which means that applying the skills we learned to process and interpret the subtleties of relating to clients—noting implicit gestures, repetitive topics, and nonverbal communication—is no longer seen as valuable or an essential part of building a healing relationship. While not every client is a good match for every therapist due to our varying skills and personalities, permission for therapist-hopping suggests to clients that it is okay to switch without learning how to confront a deeper issue, whether it is within yourself or a relational problem with the therapist.

Many of us were trained with the idea that the connection between client and therapist is the primary predictor of progress in therapy. We feel it is critical to be visually present with our clients, even if the connection is virtual, and to recognize the healing value of *presence*. So far, there is insufficient evidence that online therapy by phone, conducted with multiple therapists for brief periods, can produce the same type of connection that many of us were trained to provide.

Social Landscape

Studies have shown a large generational gap when comparing social values (Faverio, 2022; Heys, 2024). Therefore, as therapists, it is critical for us to empathize with our clients—to continue working with younger clients, we must understand the evolving social norms that shape their world. Without this understanding, we risk missing opportunities to truly hear our clients and grasp their concerns.

We also need to be honest with ourselves about our attitudes toward this social world. Some therapists feel that their years of experience and honed skills are enough to address any issue, as long as they maintain empathy. However, if we dismiss the importance of fully understanding the social context in which our clients live, we may fail to connect with them as deeply as necessary. More concerning, without a clear understanding, we may unintentionally slip into judgment. The world of today's sixteen-year-old is vastly different from the world we knew at that age. To an extent, this is true for each generation—our parents felt the same way when we were teens—but with the advent of the internet, the speed of societal and technological change has accelerated far more rapidly than in previous historical eras.

For instance, evolving views on gender fluidity and sexuality may present a newer challenge for some therapists. Younger clients, particularly those from the LGBTQIA+ community, may expect their therapist not only to be knowledgeable but also to actively affirm their identity. If an older therapist lacks this understanding or does not demonstrate enough empathy, clients may feel misunderstood or invalidated. Younger clients often expect their therapist to be an ally—someone who shows a strong commitment to social justice, inclusivity, and advocacy for marginalized communities. Older therapists may struggle with adopting this active ally role, especially if they have not had the opportunity to fully learn about allyship or diversity in a comprehensive way.

Therapists of retirement age grew up in a culture where LGBTQIA+ peers often remained closeted, and many mental health professionals considered anything outside of heteronormative behavior as evidence of mental illness or deviance. Over time, most of us rejected those cultural and psychological views, embracing the wide range of sexual identities without judgment and celebrating human diversity.

However, the current culture has evolved rapidly in the realm of sexuality, placing diversity and its challenges at the forefront of therapeutic issues. Understanding gender fluidity, transgender treatment needs, pronoun choices, and other related issues is now essential for working with younger clients. The growing recognition and acceptance of nonbinary, transgender, and gender-fluid identities has gained significant momentum in recent years. For older therapists, these concepts may still feel unfamiliar, creating a sense of being out of step with younger clients' experiences.

Older therapists might also be less familiar with evolving terminology and struggle to keep pace with the rapidly changing lexicon. This lack of fluency in contemporary language can create barriers to effective communication. Younger clients, having grown up in an environment in which gender and sexuality are viewed as a spectrum, often champion inclusivity. Meanwhile, older therapists may have been trained in clinical environments that focused on "normative" gender and sexuality, making it more difficult for them to fully understand or support the complex experiences of modern clients. Furthermore, younger clients are increasingly embracing the concept of intersectionality, which recognizes how gender and sexuality intersect with race, class, ability, and other aspects of identity. This layered understanding may be challenging for older therapists to grasp, especially if they were trained with a more simplistic or less integrated framework.

It is okay if you do not feel the desire or energy to explore the social world of young clients, but at some point, because their world is so different from your own lived experience, it may become difficult to truly imagine their lives—at the least, you'll struggle with providing the accurate empathy needed to work effectively with them. Though there are opportunities to seek out further training in areas like technology, identity, and diversity, the rapidly changing world and demands to become better educated in so many arenas can act as a push factor toward retirement.

Some therapists we interviewed mentioned that the need to keep up with generational differences in values, cultural influences, and communication styles was a significant challenge. They expressed uncertainty about whether they could make the necessary shifts to stay in tune with clients who might be fifty years their junior. They cited several factors, including:

- **Different cultural and societal contexts:** Older therapists have lived through different historical, political, and cultural experiences than younger clients, shaping their perspectives on life, politics, relationships, philosophy, and mental health.
- **Generational differences in values and attitudes:** Values around career ambition, family structure, gender roles, and work-life balance often differ across generations. Some therapists were raised in more traditional or structured environments, while younger clients embrace more fluid, nontraditional ways of living and working. This can make it difficult to maintain a nonjudgmental stance, as these differences

can feel stark. These generational divides may create a disconnect if the therapist's values or approaches appear outdated or rigid to younger clients.

- **Technology:** Younger generations are often immersed in digital communication, social media, and virtual platforms. Older therapists, however, expressed discomfort or unfamiliarity with these modes of communication. Younger clients may expect greater flexibility in how they engage with their therapist—for example, they may prefer online sessions or text-based communication, which older therapists may not fully embrace or see as necessary.
- **Pacing and expectations:** Younger clients may seek faster results or a more dynamic, action-oriented approach to therapy, while older therapists may adopt a slower, more reflective approach. This mismatch in expectations around the pacing of therapy can sometimes lead to frustration or a sense of disconnect.
- **Challenges in relating to current issues:** Younger clients often face issues that are unique to their generation, such as navigating social media pressures, economic instability, or climate anxiety. Older therapists acknowledged that it can be difficult to relate to these challenges, particularly if they are less familiar with the trends and landscapes that shape the lives of younger people.

Expectations About Therapy

It is not just social norms that are changing. The current expectations in the United States for how therapy should work have changed. When many of us were in training, we anticipated therapy to be more psychodynamic-focused, long-term, slower-paced work. Over the course of our careers, the expectation has changed—now people anticipate that therapy goals can be accomplished quickly, sometimes in a few short sessions.

The financial side to therapy has also changed, and though insurance coverage is a boon to clients seeking to gain access to therapy, therapists can inherit an immense amount of work beyond sessions to satisfy the demands of insurance providers. These companies require excessive documentation, often bordering on confidentiality violations, which takes a great deal of time from therapists who need to get treatment approved for their clients and want to be paid for providing it. Billing demands can become overwhelming, especially for a psychotherapist in a solo private practice. The rise of health maintenance organizations to limit the number of sessions exacerbates this problem even further.

Psychotherapists are also expected to keep learning throughout their careers. It's one of the benefits of our field's requirement for continuing education, but also one of its liabilities. Intellectual stimulation is a positive factor in our interest in our career, but at what point may we say, *I know enough to do my work?* At what point do we honor the wisdom that comes with years of experience? The implicit demand of continuing education is that therapists need to learn new methodologies. It implies our acquired wisdom is not enough, regardless of our skill level. This, too, can be a push factor.

You may not want to learn another treatment modality. Your intellectual stimulation may be accomplished in other ways; you may prefer to pursue learning something new outside of your field. We both taught continuing education courses and workshops for many years of our careers, and while we value writing and teaching, we are also learning about letting go. We, too, are coming to a time when it is desirable to pursue other realms of knowledge.

We are all affected by these push factors—health or age-related decline, external demands for family time or caretaking, professional demands for insurance compliance and continuing education, and the need to keep up with changing culture or therapy methods and norms—and their impact on our younger clients. How you are affected and the degree to which it affects your practice are issues to contemplate as you prepare to retire.

Pull Factors

A manager at a continuing education company bemoaned that one of its top experts, a psychotherapist, retired from teaching to take up work in environmental conservation. The manager exclaimed, "Roland won't even come back to teach one class!" But then she laughed and continued, "I guess he meant it seriously when he said he was retiring." Roland had waited years to delve into conservation efforts in his state and did not want to divert his attention back to the field. He had done as much as he could to leave his therapeutic knowledge to others, and now he had other goals. This expert psychotherapist was pulled to fulfill a passion. The opportunity to work full time on conservation was more than another job—it was not just a lifelong interest but a strongly felt value. The time and energy devoted to a worthy cause provided him rich rewards of a different kind compared to what his career had given him.

It is much more fun to think about *pull factors*—what draws us to retire rather than what pushes us to do so. What do we long to do, look forward to, or have on our bucket list? Some of us have spent a lifetime waiting for time to do these things; others just want more time to do what we already have been doing.

Anita waited all of her career as a counselor to return to her first love, music. She now played music two or three hours per day and found opportunities to perform in assisted living and nursing homes. This was fun for her; her reward was seeing the pleasure in her audiences and achieving the excellence on her instrument that she never had time for when she was working.

Spirituality

Your pull factors don't have to be based on finding another role, skill, or job, however. One survey on aging indicated that many elders, especially those over eighty years old spend more time in prayer or meditation now than at any other time in their lives. They found it satisfied a desire to connect to something greater than themselves (Koenig, 2006). Certainly, people with religious vocations in all faiths affirm the value of prayer and meditation, as some orders of monks and nuns have for centuries committed their lives to those practices. Without time pressure, many older adults begin the practice of prayer and meditation and find it highly rewarding. Sharon, recently retired, began practicing a type of meditation with a drumming group and recently connected with a group whose members sit meditatively with dying individuals. Sharon was able to combine her personal practice with a volunteer opportunity that fulfills her spiritually.

The Desire for More Time

In retirement, you might want to experience life at a more leisurely pace or have time to do things just for fun, such as reading, dancing, creating art, traveling, pursuing hobbies, or getting outside. Having worked inside an office for so much of your career, you might want to just be *out*, whether in nature or in your city. Whether you are fulfilling a lifelong passion or retreating from structure to spontaneity, you can create a retirement life that matches your values for using your time.

It is unlikely you will know *exactly* what you want to do with each day in retirement for as long as it lasts. If you are realistic, you know you will be more active in early retirement and will develop rewarding activities as your physical energy diminishes. What should you expect? Feeling purpose in life often includes making time for good relationships, loving and being loved, and doing activities that are meaningful. Meaningful activity changes with age and ability; your life may be improved by things as simple as tending to plants, taking care of a pet, or performing at least one activity per day.

At first glance, this may not fit your idea of retirement, but stop a moment and think about it. If, every day, you are expected to be somewhere, meet someone, or talk to someone, you have a purpose to fulfill that day. We get caught up in planning a retirement that is filled with energy, but we also need to know what we want to do when our energy wanes. That is when your interest in counting bird species in your yard and reporting them to the local Audubon chapter may fulfill a sense of purpose. It might be that you will make Monday evenings your turn to start coffee at a weekly AA meeting, while Tuesday afternoons are spent with the friend who stops in to watch *Jeopardy!* with you. You can feel purpose in an obligation to be present. You may still sing in your church choir, fly model planes with friends, and attend book club. The goal of retirement may not lead to new heights of creativity or contribution. *It does not need to.* A fulfilling retired life can be a life of small joys and pleasures.

Our various personal commitments have value to ourselves and those who share them. They keep us feeling that each day we have a purpose. When I (Margaret) studied others' research on purpose, I expected to find a spiritual truth about the meaning of life. When I discovered that having an activity on the calendar helped people avoid depression and contributed a feeling of significance in elder years, a bell rang in my mind. *Having something to do—especially if it is with another person—provides direction to a day.* I had thought feeling purpose in life would require some deeply meaningful activity fraught with spiritual overtones, one that would further necessitate hours of disciplined daily meditation and prayer. I was so relieved when I realized that was not the case! There is hope for us all to live cheerful retired lives just by having something to do that we enjoy.

For a successful retirement, plan to do what you enjoy and what you value. Prior to the point of retiring, test whether the activity is what you want to pursue in retirement. We have provided ideas for how to test and evaluate the new identity you may adopt in Stage IV: Action: A New Beginning. For now, at this stage of precontemplation, begin to think about those pull factors that can draw you into a successful retirement when you are ready to let go of the work you love.

Use the *Push and Pull Factors* exercise to assess the impact of push and pull factors that may be affecting your readiness for retirement.

—Exercise—

Push and Pull Factors

Push Factors

Which *push factors* are impacting you at this time? Place a check on the following boxes that apply to you; for each issue you check off, write about the possible significance and how strongly you feel its push:

- ❒ Regulations at your place of work forcing you out sooner than you wish
- ❒ Your health
- ❒ Health concerns for a family member
- ❒ Memory loss or other evidence of your own mental decline
- ❒ The demand to keep up with new technologies, social media, and online therapy options
- ❒ Changing client expectations of the therapy process
- ❒ Changing social norms among younger clients, especially related to sexuality and gender
- ❒ Insurance and other administrative or regulation demands
- ❒ Continuing education expectations

Pull Factors

Which *pull factors* seem most likely to draw you into retirement? Place a check on the following boxes that may interest you; for each box you check off, write down some specific ideas of how you might fulfill it:

- ❒ Devote yourself to a lifelong passion
- ❒ Check items off a bucket list
- ❒ Be more meditative or spiritual
- ❒ Do more fun activities
- ❒ Spend more time outside
- ❒ Learn to do something new
- ❒ Devote more time to your relationships

Mixed Messages About Push and Pull Factors

It will help you to know your personal push and pull factors, but you will also want to be able to articulate them to others. As you begin to explore your thinking and feeling about retirement, you may get mixed messages from family, friends, and peers who have their own opinions about your choice. The messages we get from people about our retirement can be all over the map depending on their relationship to us and to their work. Some may be relevant and supportive; others may be projections of their worries or feelings about your decision to stay or leave—or perhaps their own retirement options.

Barry, a member of a psychology department faculty and part-time solo practitioner, was "asked" to step down from his teaching role with the following message: "We value the work you have done so much. Don't you think it is time to let someone else have an opportunity on the faculty?" That was distinctly, if indirectly, a dismissal—an "It's time for you to leave" message.

If you are teaching and occupying tenured positions or teaching continuing education for companies, you may get a mixed message much like Barry: *We appreciate you, but it's time to step down and let others take your spot.* You may hear some version of how it is time to let younger, fresher, or newer-on-the scene therapists have an opportunity to bring their ideas to the front of our field. Some of you who work at agencies, taking lead roles in management and supervision, might feel the same pressure to step aside. It is puzzling to simultaneously hear, "You are so wise, so experienced" and at the same time, "You should leave."

The certainty that you have contributed allows you to resolve this mixed message to your advantage: "I am wise *and* I have contributed. Now I *can* leave." Still, it may be up to you to eliminate your own confusion about whether you are really finished. In stage IV, we offer an important process that can help you decide when it is time to fully let go—knowing your legacy.

But your family and friends won't necessarily focus on your legacy. They will have their own opinions and may influence your thinking and decision process. Families may say they need your income, or you might feel the need to work if your family will have to support you in retirement. Financial pressure is one block to deciding when and how to retire. The need to earn, even when one is tired of working, robs many a psychotherapist of the luxury to choose retirement. Some therapists do not have the necessary financial security for retirement. There is simply no easy answer to that reality.

You will likely have some anxiety about giving up a paycheck. That is a common reaction, especially if you are your own sole support. Examine the messages you give yourself: Are you facing real concerns about your financial security (and that of your family)? You won't be able to move into preparation or action if you skip this important stage of contemplating retirement. This is an especially important reason to do a cost-benefit analysis on your finances and include people whose needs matter to you in the discussion to reduce their anxiety—and yours!

If your family sees your income as a benefit but not a necessity, the pressure is different. Messages may be more subtle—"Of course you should retire when you want, but we can do so much with your disposable income"—thus triggering guilt about "depriving" a family member of something they want to do or purchase. This message becomes different when your family members also say, "I wish we had more time to . . ." (Fill in the blank about what your family might want from you that is not financial.) This could be more time with your grandchildren, more time to travel, more time to be together, or other ways your partners or children want your time. Living with less income is a decision you make with your loved ones, but how they pose their opinions may conflict with your wish to retire sooner rather than later.

Time and money—often in contradiction to each other—are the complex needs our loved ones present to us. And in fact, we present them to ourselves. "I want to have time, and I want to have the security of my income."

This is when it helps to think logically and clearly about time and money. In my (Lynn's) workshops and books about the business of therapy, I find that most therapists are underinformed about money management for their practices and their personal finances. They often don't know what they earn, what they spend, or how to create a budget to depend on. They haven't thought seriously about what they will need to live comfortably in retirement. Doing a cost-benefit analysis of time versus money can clarify what you will specifically need to do to have a successful financial retirement. If you need help with this analysis, please bring in others to look at your finances and help you to plan, including an accountant and a financial adviser.

That analysis will contribute to your choice of *when* to retire, but it is not the only factor in choosing a date. You need to define your own priorities of time and money so that you can set a course of action.

Your experience with clients may create some mixed messages as well. Many of them will convey, if not in so many words, that they want you to be available—forever. Or at least until they are ready to finish treatment. Clients also notice when you appear tired, when you feel stiff getting out of a chair, or when you are forgetful. They then also convey their concerns that you are not available in those moments. You feel the pull to stay and the push to go. *I know I am showing my age* and *I can still do good work.* The cognitive dissonance evoked by knowledge of your limits is decidedly uncomfortable. You know you are not at the top of your game physically and mentally, *but* you still have the ability to do the work.

Then how do you know when the balance shifts? There is no magic age when that occurs. We all need the self-honesty to recognize the tipping point. Each of us will hit a point when it is hard to compensate for flagging energy, even with the benefits of our wisdom and experience.

—*Exercise*—

Mixed Messages

For each of the following themes, write the messages you receive from yourself and others.

Your financial security—or lack thereof:

Your time with family and friends:

Your work (e.g., number of clients, availability):

Your energy level, health, and mental sharpness:

Other:

Unexpected Considerations

Even though you have a plan, life may still pose unexpected push and pull factors. Sofia faced an unexpected financial crisis when her home flooded and the damage was not covered by insurance. She needed funds for a substantial repair. She had already begun closing her practice but wanted additional income without accepting new clients, who might reasonably expect her to work with them for years. Her solution was to establish a connection with an insurance company who referred their clients for short-term assessments and therapy after one-time traumatic events. If these clients needed more time, Sofia could refer them onward. This allowed her to finish closing her existing practice and be ready to stop working altogether by simply refusing new insurance referrals. She was able to meet her financial crisis without fully reopening her practice, allowing her to now enjoy her full retirement.

I (Margaret) was also close to completely retiring my practice. Natural attrition of my clients was coming to an end. Then the pandemic hit. Clients I had not seen, some for years, reconnected for help with pandemic anxiety. Having prepared well to end my time with these clients allowed me to clarify how to reengage with some of them for a limited time, without reopening an office or reestablishing the kind of practice I previously had. I quickly came up to speed with online therapy sessions, and for the next year, went from "nearly done" to full time—but with a time limit. Fitting this unexpected return to work into my retirement preparation, I told all the returning clients I would only be available for short-term work, establishing treatment plans that were highly focused. My former clients who had previously done good therapy work benefited from short-term work dealing with issues the pandemic triggered, and they were able to say goodbye again.

As you plan the timing of your retirement, you may get the choice of whether you can slow your pace toward retirement or quit work full stop. This depends on where you work and how much control you have over the clients you accept and how long you can see them. Many therapists gradually slow down, but eventually, keeping an office open is not financially feasible. Slowing down the hours you work might not be acceptable at an agency. All of these are factors you can plan for.

Moving Forward

In the next chapter, we will discuss how to consider some of the more complex emotional issues that make it hard to think about retirement, especially those related to how psychotherapists feel compelled to keep working and helping. If you can't imagine who you will become if you are not working anymore, the next chapter will be important to read.

—Chapter 2—

Understanding the Compulsion to Work and Help

When I (Margaret) announced my decision to retire, my friend and fellow therapist Judy shook her head and smiled her "gentle" smile, one in which I read sympathy more than empathy. "I cannot believe you are even thinking of retiring," she said. "I *love* what I do. I cannot imagine wanting to give it up."

Two things went through my mind. One was that it felt like a condescending thing to say to me. The second was more defensive: She obviously hadn't listened to my very good reasons. Her remarks triggered a mix of anger and guilt. Was I abandoning clients who needed me? Was there something wrong with me for not loving my work anymore?

How we *hear* the message from others once we announce our retirement is fodder for us as we reflect on our reasons to leave. People who are not considering retiring and may never want to retire may be genuinely confused about why a psychotherapist would walk away from a successful career. They still love what they do, as I once did—until I did not want to do it anymore.

When others had the opposite reaction to Judy and congratulated me on retiring, one of my surprising feelings was irritation. Congratulations on letting go meant I was not fulfilling my work ethic. People were no longer viewing me as a hard worker! I was surprised at my inner objection and thought to myself that walking away when I *could* stay was not something to be proud of. This was not something to be congratulated! I wanted to insist I could still work. How could I still be useful, and therefore valuable, if I was not contributing to an important cause? Would people think I was lazy and useless? I thought, maybe I *should* still work. Then no one would question my usefulness in the world.

In my case, looking at my feelings in response to Judy and others showed me how complex my emotional response to retirement was. It took some time for me to reconcile all these feelings and thoughts: defensiveness, anger, guilt, and more. But working through my reactions helped me to get more secure and settled with my rationale. I had to be okay with my choice, even if someone else did not understand it. Being able to explain why you want to retire, or, like me, how you fell out of love with your career, can help you move through precontemplation and get ready for the steps of retirement.

In spite of good reasons to slow down as we age, many factors in our relationship to work stop us from considering retirement. Carol said, "I will never retire. My life is my work as a therapist. I don't have a single hobby and wouldn't know what to do with myself if I wasn't working. I know people who say they would retire and play golf every day. Not me! I can see playing golf once a week, but I cannot imagine that game would be worth getting out of bed every day." With no willingness to even plan a possible retirement, Carol may continue working until health forces her out of her job; it also raises the specter that she may unfortunately work long after she is still at her best.

Paul won't give up his practice because "it is just who I am. My weekend days off are nice and a break to do something different in the week, but to spend every day like it was a weekend would make it seem like my life has no meaning." His identity is firmly with his work. Before he will be able to let go of the work he loves, he will have to answer the following question: *Who will I be if nothing is as meaningful as what I do at work?*

What Working Means to Therapists

When we surveyed and interviewed therapists about retirement, we heard a common refrain from those in precontemplation who were ambivalent about retirement planning. Many said some version of "I love this work. I get such good feelings from being busy, earning money, and interacting with my clients. What else would ever give me such good feelings?"

Many of us work well beyond the typical age of retirement because it feels good to be busy, to work hard, to earn money, and of course, to help others. These four ways of relating to our work can compel us to keep working:

1. Work fills our days.
2. Work becomes our vocation, calling, and identity.

3. Work satisfies a need to be productive.
4. Work gives us irreplaceable good feelings.

The first of these is an issue that is common for many careers: We spend our best energy and time on the job, at work. You might have never regarded this dedication of time and energy as a problem, and in fact, it might not be, until you think about retiring. Then it might be a stumbling block, one that prevents you from fully considering if you want or need to let go of your career.

One way to recognize this block is if you experience anxiety when you think about the word *retirement*. Unease or a sense of ambiguity about what we would do instead of working can make us retreat from the topic. We humans tend to respond to ambiguity with anxiety. The anxiety you feel may not be overwhelming or cause you physical discomfort, but it may be just enough to send your thoughts in a different direction. You veer off the topic of retirement due to your anxiety with a comforting thought of *Ah, I don't have to worry about this for a long time yet.*

If work has become your identity, then feeling affixed to your career is also a key factor in precontemplation concerns. (We explore loosening the ties to your professional identity in the next chapter.) If you are unable to define yourself in a positive or constructive way without referring to your work title or role, it's time to consider whether you need to focus on other facets of your life.

Paul considers work as valuable and weekends as less consequential. He will need to balance that assessment and begin to picture what he might do with his time if he were not in the office. He has not yet come to appreciate what weekend activities mean to him and what they say about who he is equal to his time spent at work. If he leaps into retirement without having a personal identity that feels equivalent to his work identity, he might struggle with an emotional downturn at retirement.

We all need to find a deeper appreciation of who we are in all facets of our lives, especially in order to think more clearly about retirement. Work feels good because when we are at work, we are productive. Carol values effectiveness and competence. She has no idea what to do with herself and her talents or energy when not at work. Her dilemma might have had to do with the loss of direction she felt when her children moved away, or it might reflect how she has kept her talents contained to the job, forgoing other interests. If retirement is an important change to consider and she wants to shift out of precontemplation, she could start by finding some pull factors. We all need things that we value and feel valued doing—outside of the office—to begin to move toward a "third age" in life.

As we age, even the meaning of helping begins to shift. We may already be helping those in our families, but now they may begin to help us. When my father was ninety-nine years old, he came to live with me (Lynn) to help him to transition from living on his own. He helped me too, bringing his wisdom and perspective into my life in a way he had not been able to do before. My friends imagined that I would retire to be a caregiver. But I was not ready to let go of the professional work of helping, which was, in my opinion, so different from the personal helping that I was now engaged in. I noticed myself continuing to book clients for sessions into the next year; at the same time, I was searching for other caregiving resources for my father so I could remain free to continue working.

Watching people change due to, in part, my skills and effort is a powerful stimulant. My work of being a therapist and a coach can become very habit-forming because the rewards are often so immediate, session by session. The pace and rhythm of each week easily morphs into the next week, especially when clients are seeing me for ongoing therapy and keep booking ahead, eager for the next session. It's hard to think about breaking the chain of sessions that link to each other, one after another, when working is what I know best and being helpful has become so core to my value system.

Sometimes the fabric of my caseload feels too tightly knit around me, and I wonder how to pull at threads to begin to slacken its grip. At seventy-four, I intend to work less and intentionally remove days from my calendar each week to have clear breaks in my schedule. This loosens the weave of my caseload's tapestry and lets in more air and breathing room. I also screen what new clients I will see and refer out those whose treatment requires more of a commitment of time or intensity than I think is right for me to offer now. Another set of threads released. Within another year, using this metaphor, my tapestry could look even more open; I like to think it could be varied, colorful, and intricate, with larger open gaps and long threads dangling, letting in daylight. Perhaps this is how my work calendar will unravel over time if I intentionally keep letting in more and more light—it will become less a knit and more a transparent lace.

—Exercise—

Relating to Your Work

Answer the following questions to determine how you relate to your work.

How do you think and feel about each of the four ways you might relate to your work?

1. Work fills my days:

____

____

____

____

2. Work has become my vocation, calling, and identity:

____

____

____

____

3. Work satisfies a need to be productive:

____

____

____

____

4. Work gives me irreplaceable good feelings:

____

____

____

____

Which of these four ways of relating to your work is most familiar to you and why?

What, if anything, do you want to shift or change in order to begin to prepare for an approaching retirement?

What metaphor could you use to describe your relationship between your work and yourself?

When Working Becomes Compulsive

What I (Margaret) thought of as a positive work ethic was probably closer to a compulsion to work. I chose my career based on a desire to help others, a value I carry to this day, but underneath that I also had a deep need to be useful in some way. I had been raised with the model of hard work equating to goodness or value. I took it to heart without ever reflecting much on what that would mean if I quit working. If I was to retire without distress, I had to construct my sense of worth around something other than just being a hard worker.

Basing my self-worth on my productivity wasn't a big problem when I was still working; I was working as many hours as suited me. As a single woman with grown children, I could work as I chose and at my discretion. I needed to work hard to save for retirement. As a solo practitioner, every hour I worked increased my income, which fueled my blindness to the emotional or physical impact of extra hours in the office. Financial need also prevented me from looking at the other reasons for constant work. Despite always carrying a full caseload of clients, I also chose to spend as much as six days a month traveling to teach continuing education. I spent my time off writing books. I was productive and useful, and I loved it.

You might read this and think "work addiction" was my problem. Yes, I was darned close to it. I was a former addictions counselor and I knew the signs, so I had to look at myself through that lens. As so often happens, especially for women, when I was newly divorced, I was broke. I had two young children and was going through graduate school. I had to work hard—and constantly. I prided myself on my energy to do it. Even a brief emotional collapse as I finished my degree did not disabuse me of the notion that I could work without replenishment.

Our finances may make us feel compelled to work. Some therapists, even though they're at a late stage in their careers, may conclude that working as long as possible is necessary. Erma knew she would need to work full time until she is eighty, if she remains able, to pay off the mortgage on her house and other debts. She was financially wiped out by a one-two punch of her husband incurring medical expenses and losing his business. He could no longer contribute to their finances, and Erma needed to make sure they had enough money to live on as they grew older.

Working hard and working for a long time without thinking about retirement does not mean you have a compulsion. It may be a preference, a survival strategy, or a choice. But sometimes when we talk to those who could retire and feel anxious to even explore the idea, we see that working and helping can be a compulsion or even an addiction.

Work Addiction

Work addiction is rarely predicated on financial need. Work addiction, like other addictions, usually results in damaged relationships, and it isolates the addict from normal, ordinary experiences. Those with this addiction lose the ability to experience activities that are fun or relaxing without intense discomfort from being away from their work. Modern technology intensifies work addiction; cell phones and Wi-Fi availability allow work addicts to stay online and able to be contacted at all times.

Although I (Margaret) did not cross the threshold for addiction, it was close for me. I worked full time, if not overtime, as I neared retirement. I did have the ability to enjoy time off with friends, but when the time came for me to walk away from work, I was not prepared for what daily life would be like. My self-worth was reliant on working. What would replace that?

Without daily demands, I struggled to keep track of days without a predictable schedule. I still wanted to be important and useful, and I threw myself into volunteering and other activities at a pace that rivaled my work hours, thinking that would solve the problem of the schedule. The frenetic pace of activity with a single organizing frame—a career—quickly made me realize I needed to revisit the contemplation stage and think through what pulled me to retire.

If you see yourself in the dilemma of needing work to feel direction in your life—if you are uncomfortable with days that have no demands—you can contemplate what pull factors will feel meaningful to you. You can prepare to replace busyness with, perhaps, less busyness, but also with activities that utilize your abilities in new, refreshing ways.

RETIREMENT JOURNAL

Your Feelings About Working

Think further about your feelings regarding work by answering the following prompts in your retirement journal:

- Does your work ethic demand that you work full time?
- How does your work ethic dictate that if you retire, you will maintain some work that you can tell others about? (e.g., *I am still valuable because I still do . . .*)
- How many hours have you been working? What will replace those hours?
- What would you do with hours that are empty of demands?
- What activities that you do now are fun for you?
- Will you be able to talk with pride about those activities when you retire?

Needing to Help

If you are like most therapists, your career reflects your values, your beliefs, and your ideal self. As one of our interviewees put it, "I chose this profession because I wanted to help people live better lives." Being a psychotherapist often means being a giver. It is in our nature to give to people who need us—our compassion, our expertise, our presence—and it feels great to have those qualities to offer.

Our relationships with our clients are real, but they are primarily one-directional. They are not mutual, and what we get back is not the same as what we give. A therapist's major sense of reward comes from seeing people make positive changes. If you are feeling some guilt about retiring, consider whether it is related to this: Do you think that by retiring, you are denying current and future clients the resources and help you could give if you stayed? If you take yourself out of the equation, do you feel that you deny your clients what they need?

—*Exercise*—

Tracking Your Need to Help

Answer the following questions to determine whether you feel comfortable with the decision to stop helping others in a professional role.

When you talk about retiring, how do you feel when others say, "How can you leave when what you do is so valuable?"

How do you react when other therapists comment, "I cannot even imagine not working—it is so rewarding"?

Do you hear an implication that you are making a mistake and will regret quitting?

Do you feel guilty about leaving specific clients?

What is it that those individuals need from you?

What specific talents and skills will you take from your clients if you retire?

Can these clients get those needs met by anyone else, even if it may take them some time to form the trust or the relationship that you have established with them?

Compassion Addiction

Many therapists feel compelled to keep helping and giving, extending themselves beyond their own limits and expressing the belief that they *must* do so. Nancy said she could not consider retiring and walking away from the people who needed her, despite the fact that she knew she was not taking good care of her health. She envied experiences her friends were enjoying, especially one who took an extended trip with her partner and another who was learning pickleball with a group of neighbors. They were bonding and having fun—without her. She acknowledged wishing for the time and the fun her friends were having with each other, but her work was too important to replace with fun and relaxation. Her clients needed her help too much for her to leave them.

She thought about signing up for an evening yoga class, but admitted, "I need the exercise, and that would be a relaxing way to add it into my life, but I just cannot take nights away from the office. Too many of my clients need to see me in the evening." Nancy saw herself as being a "savior" for her clients. When asked whether she *needed* to be a savior, she was stymied. "This is what I do. I am their protector. I feel certain about this."

Nancy voices an important but rarely discussed problem for those who have a career of helping: the slippery slope when helping others becomes compassion addiction. It might seem odd to include a discussion about compassion addiction in a book about retirement. However, if you feel a visceral reluctance to retire, consider the possibility that you have come to rely on your work to create good feelings in your life. You might be thrown into a state of withdrawal if you are not aware of the emotional and physical power of the state of compassion addiction.

But how can feeling compassion become an *addiction*? Compare it to a general definition of addiction: Addictions begin because you get a good feeling when you ingest a substance or engage in a behavior. Addiction is evident when you continue to do it even when doing so hurts you in some way.

The feel-good nature of compassion is like that. When you do anything that feels good, your brain releases a substance called *dopamine*. Dopamine activates the reward network in your brain so your physical and emotional responses are pleasurable; this reinforces the behavior. It feels good when a client thanks you or when you know you had a great session. Dopamine flows and you happily return to work. Another good session will reinforce work as a great way to feel good.

When you are compassionate to others, you also get a hit of *oxytocin*, a bonding neurochemical that makes you feel close to your clients. Oxytocin flows when you have positive physical touch, but also when you experience joy, delight, or comfort with another person. You feel good because they feel good. Oxytocin makes it certain you want to interact with that person again. Between the oxytocin and the dopamine, you have a warm, fuzzy, very good feeling.

—Exercise—

The Rewards of Compassion

Answer the following questions to explore how being compassionate is fulfilling for you.

What are five feelings you get from working with people who need your help?

1. ______________________________
2. ______________________________
3. ______________________________
4. ______________________________
5. ______________________________

In considering each of the feelings you listed, how long does each one last?

1. ______________________________
2. ______________________________
3. ______________________________
4. ______________________________
5. ______________________________

When was the first time you remember having these feelings (at any age and not necessarily related to work)?

1. ______________________________
2. ______________________________
3. ______________________________

4. ______________________________

5. ______________________________

In what other nonwork places, situations, or activities do you have these feelings? How long do they last?

1. ______________________________
2. ______________________________
3. ______________________________
4. ______________________________
5. ______________________________

Anyone who feels this good about their work will miss it when they let it go. However, when compassion feels *good*, so good that you might derive more good feelings from work than from any other activity, you are going to be hard pressed to replace it.

Without activities that stimulate dopamine and oxytocin, you may experience excessive loss and grief when you retire. You might find yourself feeling depressed, and you may, without preparation, wander through each day feeling irritable or even aimless. In turn, you may crave ways to feel as good as you did. If you are not deriving good feelings from any other activities besides work, you will miss it even more in retirement.

RETIREMENT JOURNAL

Recognizing Compassion Addiction

Consider how you have used compassion in your career by reflecting on the following prompts in your retirement journal:

- Have you had the experience of missing your work?
- Do you get irritable and defensive when discussing retirement, as if you are being accused of laziness or lack of compassion?
- Why would contemplating retirement bring up regret, guilt, or irritation when it seems like the right decision to retire?
- What are the areas of retired life in which you can expect to live out your values to compassionately give to others?

Compassion Fatigue

As givers, we know we thrive on compassion and helping others, but we also know that our work can cause compassion fatigue. Although we are trained to listen in a way that protects us from absorbing the trauma of our clients, secondary trauma is a concern for those in our profession. Staying emotionally balanced is not easy when your client's history mirrors your own or when you are deeply empathic with their traumatic experiences. Although all therapists strive to understand clients from their perspective, empathizing with clients who have suffered enormously exposes therapists to vicarious suffering.

To avoid compassion fatigue, therapists must find ways to recharge and keep balance in their lives. To manage the stress of this work, you need collegial support, sufficient time to get the work done, and the right resources to stay effective and present with clients. Without that support, even the reward of helping is insufficient to deal with the stress of treatment. You can become tired in a way that demands rejuvenation.

How would you recognize compassion fatigue? It feels similar to stress, but it is ongoing. It is also similar to depression, but often without an obvious source. Emotional signs include anxiety and sadness, and physical signals may show up as tiredness, digestive problems, and headaches. You may also feel like you have less energy for your significant relationships—being irritable, disinterested, and emotionally unavailable. If you recognize yourself in the description of compassion fatigue, you are not alone.

RETIREMENT JOURNAL

Compassion Fatigue Recovery

If you are someone who has suffered compassion fatigue, consider the following prompts for ways you might restore yourself, perhaps even well enough to avoid serious compassion fatigue:

- What helps you to recover?
- Do you take time away from the office?
- Does obtaining your own psychotherapy help to get yourself back on track?
- Do you take extended time off—a long vacation or a work hiatus—before you feel the energy to return to your work?
- How can you change your routine? (e.g., add in time for self-care like exercise, more sleep, or more fun)

Getting the "High" in Retirement

If we are part of something that provides us with such joy and self-worth, there may not seem like many good reasons to leave it. Reflect on how you feel after a powerful, helpful session in which you knew you were insightful and supported your client. She walked away from her drunk husband without arguing. You had worked with her for months to see how his behavior affected her mood, and how little influence her arguing had over his drinking. She tearfully tells you how grateful she is, and she feels so much self-esteem from that action of self-care. You helped her see how self-control is different from not caring about him. Whew! And then she did it! Woo-hoo!

Your feelings after session like this are not only joy on your clients' behalf, but more. You feel good about your values being played out in your work. This happens regularly, and you have become used to the upside of helping, the dopamine and oxytocin boost.

When you retire, you will miss those good feelings and will need to replace them. As you get ready to retire, contemplation should include examining your relationship to your work so you can prepare to move smoothly into a new level of activity. When you prepare to retire, you will want a plan for how to replace that "high" when you no longer have work to provide it.

Now consider this: Can you find this same joy and reward of helping outside of work? Are there ways you can get positive feelings from other sources? Is helping others in your role the only way to feel this good about yourself? Consider these questions in the following prompts and note your answers in your retirement journal.

RETIREMENT JOURNAL

Finding Other Sources of Rewards

Return to the *Rewards of Compassion* exercise and copy down your answers to the final question. Then reflect on the following prompts in your retirement journal:

- In what other non-work-related places, situations, or activities do you have similar rewarding feelings? How long do they last?

  1. ______________________________
  2. ______________________________
  3. ______________________________
  4. ______________________________
  5. ______________________________

- When will you or do you tend to engage in these activities?
- Can you commit to doing more to have these rewarding feelings outside of work?
- The next time you are in these situations, review your experience, noting how you felt before and after.

Moving Forward

As you begin to think more about how to let go of the work you love, you can be intentional in adding activities to retirement that will replace the rewards of helping others in the office while still allowing you to use your values, skills, and talents. In the next chapter, we will focus on another step in precontemplation stage: how to loosen the ties of your professional identity and develop a sense of self that is separate and distinct from your work persona. It can be easier to step away from a long career when you know who you will be and what you will enjoy.

—Chapter 3—

Loosening the Ties to Your Professional Identity

After publishing my first book on the business of therapy, I (Lynn) spent decades teaching therapists how to build and sustain their practices. Given that over 70 percent of therapists will spend some time in private practice during their careers, they need solid business skills to thrive. The biggest challenge, however, was teaching them how to talk about themselves publicly. Therapists, who excel in reflection and listening, frequently struggle with marketing—often viewing it as inauthentic or promotional. And for good reason. Our work is rooted in genuine relationships, and we strive to make those connections compassionate and real from the very first hello.

In order to build their practices, therapists have to demystify therapy as they explain their methods and services. It is a struggle for many to find the right words to explain who they are, what they offer, and why it matters. Over time, marketing strategies have morphed into what we call *branding* (Grodzki, 2015). As marketer Seth Godin (2018) explains, a brand is the set of expectations, memories, stories, and relationships that, taken together, account for a client's decision to choose one service over another.

Gradually, therapists have learned to build their own personal brands—which I explain in my book as the brand called "you" (Grodzki, 2015). In today's culture, many therapists create websites that highlight not just their services, but also their values, bios, and philosophies on healing and treatment. They write blogs and use social media to increase their visibility in a crowded marketplace. They also develop skills in networking, outreach, and cultivating a public persona.

But marketing is not the only thing that keeps therapists focused on their professional lives. Most pursue extensive clinical training on a continual basis at their own expense to refine their expertise. They get supervised outside of clinical hours to improve their outcomes, and many do this for the entirety of their career. Treating a complex caseload, handling administrative demands, continually training to improve skills, studying, getting supervision, networking, and doing outreach—most therapists live and breathe their work. No wonder they develop a strong sense of professional focus and identity.

Building a strong professional identity is necessary for a therapist in a variety of roles, but it has both an upside and a downside. For those considering retirement, the downside of intense professional emphasis is that a professional identity can dominate a personal sense of self.

The process of retirement presents an opportunity to rebalance multiple identities. To retire from the "brand called you" means finding a way to unhook from a professional identity to attend to other parts of self.

Parts of Self

To encourage those in precontemplation to explore their multiple identities, we query those in our workshops: Can you describe yourself apart from your professional role? How will you define your worth without your license, degree, or title preceding your name? If you take away the brand, the elevator pitch, the website, the public persona—who are you then?

And perhaps most importantly: How will it feel to stand free of your professional identity and fully engage with the next phase of your life?

Oriah Mountain Dreamer (2006) has a provocative inquiry in the first line of her poem "The Invitation": "It doesn't interest me what you do for a living. I want to know what you ache for and if you dare to dream of meeting your heart's longing." As you approach retirement, you too may become less interested in what you are doing for a living and begin to explore other subtle longings.

We wondered about the ongoing process of separating the ties of professional and personal identities when we sent out surveys to therapists in the process of retirement. The first question we asked was *How do you describe yourself?* The overwhelming majority of respondents answered by stating their licensure, job title, or specialty areas in their work as a therapist. They pointed to their professional role before any other personal definition.

—*Exercise*—

Your Identity

Answer the following questions to understand your current identity.

A new acquaintance says, "Tell me about yourself." Write the first five things that come to mind.

1. ____
2. ____
3. ____
4. ____
5. ____

How many of these are related to your work? Did you use a title or position that you hold? Did you talk about your education?

Reflect on how you chose your career.

What did this say about you then?

What does this say about you now?

What are the different hats you wear?

What are your clinical strengths?

What are your professional strengths?

What are your personal strengths?

How would your colleagues describe you?

How would your friends or family describe you?

Unpacking the Meaning of Your Professional Identity

Since we pack so much into our professional identity, it can help to sort through what your identity means to you as you start to unravel the components of your working role. Professional identity often comprises several factors, including:

- Values
- Knowledge
- Beliefs
- Skills
- Status

For example, what are your core values? Are they equally present in both your work and your personal life? If not, start to think about how and where your values are best expressed. Do you live your values more at work than during nonwork time? How do your values inform your time at home or with friends and family?

Then consider your knowledge base. What knowledge and experience fuels your work? Will you continue to use this intelligence after you retire? How about your beliefs: Which beliefs guide your work? Do you leave them in the office at the end of a working day, or do they stay with you in all that you do during your nonworking time?

Will the skills you have honed stay intact in retirement? Is there a place for your skills in other aspects of your nonwork life? If your expertise doesn't factor in your retirement plans, will that feel like a loss?

Perhaps the hardest aspect on the list to sort out is that of status. Even when retirement is a desired life change, letting go of one's licensure, title, position, business, or leadership role can be bittersweet. If your designation changes when you retire, will it feel like freedom or like a demotion?

Ginny is in solo private practice as a psychologist and nearing retirement. "I have about another year left in me to practice and then I want to stop. I see kids, and they and their parents all call me Dr. Ginny. Just like Dr. Phil and Dr. Ruth! The hardest thing for me? To no longer be Dr. Ginny."

Ginny is proud of the time and effort she has devoted to achieving her degree; accepting a loss of her title due to retirement was formidable. Like many of her age, Ginny represents a large cohort of therapists that are now headed for retirement—baby boomers who were pioneers in their ability to enter a once male-dominated profession. Their master and doctoral degrees were hard-won; they fought to have independence, the ability to diagnose and treat clients, and self-determination in the ways that they worked.

For some, the loss of status means a loss of leadership. Audrey rose from being a staff counselor to become an executive director of a large mental health foundation. "Even though I don't have an MBA, my master's degree in counseling was flexible and valued in my position because I have good people skills and communication. I loved having my own office with a title on the door. I am so proud of the work I do with my team. I hate giving up the standing and influence that this role has conferred," she said.

Audrey explained that after being an executive director with a staff to manage, her professional identity of being the boss was indistinguishable from her personal definition. She likened it to two trees growing together side by side. The longer she stayed in her role, the more the trees' roots intercrossed and became tangled together. She thought that the two personalities or identities complemented each other, and even though they would need to separate somewhat when she retired, she felt confident that she would still be much the same person.

But she was still worried about the shift in identity. "I will go from leading a team, and knowing literally thousands of people all around the country from decades of attending conferences, to being . . . well, I guess . . . just me."

It takes time to untangle the roots, to contemplate what belongs to the job and what belongs to you. To let go of the status of your role, you may need to name and claim the values, knowledge, beliefs, and skills that belong to you as a whole person, not just to your title. Defining the "just me" aspect of self is an important task as you move through readiness during precontemplation.

RETIREMENT JOURNAL

"Just Me" Self-Definition

It can be helpful to define what you truly mean by "just me." Allow yourself to remember or reclaim additional aspects of your nonwork identity by answering the following prompts in your retirement journal:

- What did you want to be when you were a child, teenager, or young adult?
- How do you like to relax when you have unstructured time?

- What was the best (nonwork) book you read this year? What did you take away that was important to you?
- Who inspires you? Why?
- What was the biggest (nonwork) adventure in your life? How did it affect you?
- When was the last time you took a risk? How did it turn out?
- What makes you laugh?
- Who are your best friends?
- What principles guide you in life?
- When do you feel most like your best self?
- What does success mean to you?

Reclaim Your Personal Identity

Do you notice a slight shift in your bearing when you unlock your office door and step inside? Do you straighten your shoulders or banish a smile? For some therapists, the individual you become when you are in your chair may not be the most natural part of yourself. To fit into your professional role, there may be instinctive parts of you that you have had to minimize, mute, or discount.

For example, I (Lynn) am naturally directive and can be pointed in my responses. I get amused easily and often laugh out loud in conversation. I tend to self-disclose. These are traits that I exhibit in my personal life, but they certainly didn't fit into the methods of psychodynamic psychotherapy in which I was originally trained. In my master's program, I learned to be more of a blank screen, to stay empathic but not amused, and I tamped down the barbed quips and self-disclosure. This made sense, and of course I wanted to learn to be a good clinician. But over time, I noticed that the longer I worked as a therapist using this method, the more I became a blander version of myself. Even when I was not working, I became quieter, less outspoken, more self-reflective, and less reactive. This was not a bad thing, but it meant that some of the spark and fun of my personality was lessening due to the hours spent working within a different persona.

I (Margaret) am naturally reflective and somewhat serious in personality. I always wanted to be an actor and studied theater in college. As an actor, I was insatiably curious about what motivated the people I portrayed on stage. Ironically,

I was raised in a family where asking questions of others was considered rude; curiosity about another person might cause them discomfort. So theater gave me a place to be myself, to question and explore. I knew by the time I graduated that I was not destined to be an actor, and as I discovered psychotherapy as a career, I found my interest in motivation was a good match. However, in my early training, I—not my clients—was the one that was more uncomfortable with questioning, which felt to me like going against my family's rules about curiosity. My role allowed me to grow and learn that others need the curiosity and attention of their therapist to hear themselves. As I started to provide continuing education trainings, my acting experience came in handy, and the playful, creative, dramatic side of myself found a place to be expressed.

Have you noticed a shift in aspects of your personality that you have had to make in order to be successful in your professional role?

Jed said that as a younger man, during his PhD courses, he saw himself as having a helpful and compassionate style of asking questions and having deep curiosity about others. But after graduation, in the therapeutic milieu where he worked, he had to assume a much more distant, observing analytic stance to be successful. He said it actually aged him, made him seem wise and serious—a good thing when he was young, as he wanted to be taken seriously by his colleagues and clients. But now, as he prepares to retire, he said he wishes he could find the younger part of his self that he has suppressed. Now he wants to feel younger, lighter, and more playful.

You may have felt you needed to hide some aspects of your personality to maintain a professional identity, including your age, gender focus, or sexual orientation; due to the community or agency in which you worked, it may have felt safer to avoid opening up. There may also be emotional reactions you needed to contain or aspects of yourself, including your religion, language, or ethnicity, that you felt you needed to de-emphasize. This was likely done in the service of doing the work, but it was at a high cost to your sense of self.

Carl Jung wrote much about persona, indicating that it is not appropriate to show all of who we are in every relationship or setting. You may have found yourself in a situation similar to the one we, your authors, did. We could be completely genuine in the part of our identity we revealed to clients; however, we couldn't reveal all of ourselves, and the strain of withholding important aspects of your identity can be painful.

Berry, a therapist and clinical director at a nonprofit agency, said that she has a strong sense of social justice and resonates with the idea of being a "citizen therapist" to leverage community change into her treatment. However, the agency she works for has told her that this is not their policy or mandate. She has been at her agency for over twenty years and will finish out her career there, but once retired, she looks forward to being more of her full self. "I want to be free to stand up for the causes I believe in. It's sad that I need to retire in order to reclaim this important part of myself."

In an earlier example, we saw that Audrey had a positive experience of combining her professional and personal "tree roots," and she considered both identities to be woven together in a complementary way. This is the best outcome, when both identities are well balanced. If your professional and personal identities are out of balance or misaligned however, merging them has been shown to decrease the sense of well-being and lessen productivity. Research suggests that, over time, your professional identity, whatever it may be, becomes the dominant personality, if you spend the majority of your time and energy working. Adherence to a misaligned professional identity can alter your innate personality traits (Miscenko & Day, 2016).

As you work through the exercises in this chapter, it may occur to you that we all have multiple identities, some that are given to us and others that we build in various situations. These identities shift in a dynamic process, one that lasts through various life stages, including the changes brought on by retirement. You are an individual and you are distinct, but your life is in flux. As you retire, you will be making new meaning about who you are, where you belong, and what matters to you.

We encourage you to think about your many possible identities and how they relate to your goals and dreams in retirement. Some research suggests that the experience of holding multiple identities that need to shift and adjust over time can be good for mental health—especially when these identities allow for connection with others: the more social identifications, the higher the sense of well-being (Manzi et al., 2023).

Walt Whitman's (1892/2023) poem "Song of Myself" contains the famous line "I contain multitudes." This speaks to the ability to have an expanded sense of self, one that takes from each experience to weave a greater tapestry. The opportunity in the precontemplation stage of retirement is to gently untangle your multiple identities, to rebalance and even reclaim the parts of your personality that you want and need for the next phase of your life.

—*Exercise*—

Rebalance Your Multiple Identities

If you need to rebalance or separate your multiple work and nonwork identities, try these steps:

1. **Realign concealed or misaligned parts:** Review the following list of parts of self that may not exist fully in your professional persona. Check off the aspects of yourself that you have had to diminish to perform your work role:

   - ❒ Age
   - ❒ Ability
   - ❒ Emotions
   - ❒ Physicality
   - ❒ Gender
   - ❒ Strength
   - ❒ Political beliefs
   - ❒ Religion
   - ❒ Sexual orientation
   - ❒ Relationship or parenting status
   - ❒ Ethnicity
   - ❒ Culture
   - ❒ Native language
   - ❒ Other: ____________

   Now decide how you might honor and promote these aspects in order to rebalance or realign your innate personality. What steps will you take to do this? How might it benefit you over time? What part can it play in your thinking about retirement?

   ____

   ____

   ____

   ____

   ____

   ____

   ____

2. **Renew your social circle outside of work:** Who do you spend time with that can encourage and promote the realigned parts of self, to help you stay separate from your office identity?

   ___

   ___

   ___

   How could you improve or enhance your nonwork social circle?

   ___

   ___

   ___

3. **Take space:** How can you create an environment to support this shift in alignment? Do you need time alone? Time in nature? Time with others? Can you take space to explore creative endeavors, movement, or adventures? Would it help to set aside space for long chats with friends who know other parts of you? Can you add some formal meditation time as a way to be quiet and listen to your internal voices, longings, and needs? Will you plan spontaneous excursions, or allow yourself time to experiment with new activities?

   I will take space for myself to reaffirm my personal identity by including these practices, routines, or rituals on a regular basis:

   ___

   ___

   ___

   ___

   ___

   ___

   ___

Moving Forward

You have now completed the three chapters in the stage of precontemplation. After looking at some of the obstacles you need to overcome in order to think and plan for a good retirement, you may start to shift into the next stage of the Readiness for Retirement Model: Contemplation.

In contemplation, we explore the unique complexities of retirement, particularly the challenge of preparing our clients for our departure. One of the greatest challenges for therapists is knowing how to end relationships well with those who rely on us for their well-being. In chapter 4, you'll discover why endings in therapy can be difficult, how to increase your self-awareness and stay centered, and how to create a constructive process for both yourself and the clients who depend on your skills and services.

Stage II

Contemplation: The Therapeutic Conversation

As a therapist, you are often a lifeline for those who rely on your services, and the therapeutic relationship you've built may not be easily replaceable. Moving into the *contemplation stage* of retirement means carefully considering how to end treatment, especially when the decision to end is not the client's choice. This type of ending, one that is initiated by the therapist, is also known in psychological terminology as a *forced ending*, and it requires thoughtful planning and attention to ensure that your clients' needs are met and their well-being is not compromised.

In the next three chapters, you'll find explanations and exercises designed to help you understand why endings in therapy are complex and how to navigate them thoughtfully. Contemplation involves clarifying your clinical philosophy, which will guide your process of letting go. You'll explore concepts and tools to understand the dynamics of attachment in endings, both for clients and therapists. This section includes exercises and journaling prompts to help you first explore your own feelings about endings so that your leave-takings with clients can be positive, constructive, and compassionate.

—Chapter 4—

Why Endings in Therapy Are Difficult

Most therapists learn early how to start and maintain a practice, but few of us have had more than a cursory education or supervision to know how to end one. We are focused on how to help clients begin treatment, but not much on how to help them finish. Even if we have been taught some termination principles, endings as they happen in the real world may not follow suit. In therapy, as in life, many endings happen unilaterally (e.g., the client chooses to end treatment) and without our advance planning (e.g., the client gets a promotion and moves away hurriedly mid-treatment), or the treatment halts without a chance to determine its success or failure.

Whether we offer long-term ongoing psychoanalytic therapy or brief six-session anger management, most of us are not trained to help our clients leave us with a sense of completion and confidence. We don't regularly provide clients with a set of steps of leaving, at least not in the same way that we establish the outset of their treatment plans. We don't know how to design an *intentional* ending in therapy—one that is mutually planned and agreed upon between us and the client—that supports the work of healing that has taken place, and that is complete and constructive. The steps to ending a therapeutic relationship well are often a mystery for both the client and the therapist.

I (Lynn) recall a difficult ending in my own long-term individual therapy. It was my choice to end, but it was fraught with struggle. I had been in individual and group therapy with "M" twice a week for twenty years. Not only was she my therapist, but she was also my mentor who'd helped me take the leap to become a therapist myself. I was very attached to her and all she did for me. When I decided I was ready to leave therapy, I announced this to her, saying I wanted to give myself a year to end. Giving a year's notice seemed reasonable and respectful for the work we had done together. I asked what she thought I should focus on to end my work with her. She was silent and then said that the last piece of work for me was to deal with my relationship with her.

I was taken aback and unsure of how to proceed. The topic was unprocessed—how I felt about her and how I thought she felt about me—and it was full of unresolved issues. Did she really like and approve of me after all this time? Had I been honest about my thoughts and judgments of her? Her analytic stance left much of the process up to me, and trying to dissect our relationship felt like undergoing another full course of therapy. I had projected so much of my personal history and emotion onto her, yet there was no clear path to making sense of it all, no guidance on how to approach termination. Left largely to navigate it alone, I ended up floundering through the sessions, cycling through waves of grief, loss, anger, and betrayal. It was, in the end, a miserable year. Although I was a therapist with my own practice by then, I felt adrift, with no sense of direction or clarity about whether the turmoil I was experiencing during the ending was normal or even valid. When I finally left, I was exhausted and relieved to be done—not the closure I had hoped for or expected. Without clear direction in where the ending was going, she may have been as lost as I was. Endings in therapy can be muddled if there is little guidance from the therapist.

Looking back, I now have more compassion for what happened. Most therapists aren't trained to end well. It didn't matter that I was the one leaving rather than being left—I had no personal experience to draw on when it came to creating a healthy ending to a close relationship. My history was marked more by failed relationships than by successful closures. As you read through this section and reflect on the stage of contemplation, we'll guide you in creating more constructive and compassionate relational endings as you approach retirement.

In your retirement journal, briefly review your own history of endings in both your personal and your professional life. Use the following prompts to assess your own experience of endings, noting your patterns or blind spots. You may develop more insight about how you have tended to end relationships or have them ended for you.

RETIREMENT JOURNAL

Your History of Endings

Discover your intention to see endings from a safer and more secure point of view by reflecting on the following prompts in your retirement journal:

- What close, personal, intimate relationships have ended in your personal life or in your professional career?
- Who ended the relationship, you or the other person?
- Were you prepared for the ending?
- If you initiated the ending, what was your process of leaving?
- If the other person initiated the ending, what was the process of ending like?
- Do you see a pattern with how people have ended relationships with you?
- Do you see a pattern of how you end relationships?
- If so, what do the patterns suggest?
- In a perfect world, what would you have wanted from these endings to have a better outcome for you or for the other person?

Therapist-Initiated Forced Endings

When a therapist prepares to retire and announces the end of treatment, they initiate a process of closure known in professional terms as a *forced ending* (or imposed ending). While the conclusion of therapy can often be a positive and constructive experience for clients, the decision, in this case, is made solely by the therapist for their own reasons, leaving the client with no choice in the matter. This lack of agency may make the ending feel abrupt or out of the client's control.

Because the therapist who is retiring determines when treatment concludes—based on their personal needs or circumstances—this decision may conflict with the client's needs and desires. As a result, clients may experience feelings of rejection, abandonment, or even an unspoken breach of trust, especially if they had expected the therapist's involvement until therapy felt complete to them. While endings in therapy are often complex, those imposed or initiated by the therapist can be particularly challenging for both therapist and client to navigate.

This imposed ending of treatment may cause significant anxiety and worry for clients once it is announced. However, prior to the announcement, it can also be deeply upsetting for the therapist to even consider. When clients are dependent on your treatment, view you as a vital lifeline, or have formed a strong rapport and connection with you through your therapeutic work, the prospect of announcing an end to therapy can be emotionally wrenching. Ending therapy well requires a thoughtful and considerate approach. The two of us have discussed how best to refer to these types of endings. The term *forced ending* may carry a harsh connotation, and our goal is to ensure that the ending you create with your clients is collaborative and ultimately a positive transition. However, because *forced* is the term that most therapists use and understand, we are choosing to keep that part of this larger discussion about endings.

We propose that there are three steps to best handle a process of therapist-initiated forced endings in therapy. These include 1) staying grounded and secure inside yourself, 2) understanding and anticipating the depth of client attachment, and 3) handling your own reactions, process, or countertransference. The first step will be addressed in this chapter, and the second and third steps will be discussed in chapters 5 and 6, respectively.

Three-Step Plan for Therapist-Initiated Forced Endings

1. **Practice staying grounded and secure inside yourself.**
2. Understand client attachment and help clients process their anger, pain, grief, or loss by staying present, responsive, and empathic.
3. Recognize your own reactions and process in ending.

Staying Grounded

Let's begin with step one: staying grounded. The first step to ending well is taking the time to prepare yourself so that you feel certain that your decision is right for you. In the next chapter, we'll explore how to prepare your *clients* for a forced ending. But first, it's essential that you process your *own* feelings, thoughts, and concerns independently so they don't interfere with your clients' experience.

For example, you might be retiring while managing a full caseload, breaking the news to dozens of clients. If you lead a team or manage others, they may also have reactions and feelings about your retirement that are akin to how a client feels. In this situation, it's crucial to stay steady, empathetic, and patient with the disruption that your decision will create. This is understandably stressful and challenging. So, how can you maintain a sense of inner security when your clients' distress—session after session—feels tied to your decision to retire?

Ideally, before you begin the ending process, you'll take time to reflect, practice, and plan for internal steadiness. You'll want to stay calm, nonreactive, and positive when you make your announcement and all the way until your client's treatment draws to a close. By doing so, you can model secure attachment, offering your clients a sense of safety as they navigate their own process of ending.

In discussing secure attachment, Winnicott (1991) explained, a parent can look away, be distracted, or allow the child to experience frustration or disappointment, but the overall parenting is sufficient for the emergence of an emotionally and psychologically healthy child. A parent can fail in tolerable ways. Therefore, having a secure attachment is akin to being a "good enough mother," whereby you provide a therapeutic holding environment in a session. You are attentive and calm, but you are not required to be perfect.

A therapist can handle endings well, but it's important to recognize that some missteps are inevitable and not necessarily catastrophic. Perfection isn't the goal. What matters most is starting with a grounded, safe presence when you announce the news. By doing so, you help create an environment where clients can sense safety and comfort as they process the news themselves.

Identify and work through your emotions about ending ahead of time. Then you can encourage your clients to explore their own emotions without being triggered. You want to stay empathic and compassionate as they talk about you leaving and what it will mean for them, but you will also hold your boundaries and let any client's reactions be theirs alone. You can be nonreactive as you provide the holding environment to contain the experience for their security and safety. You can be present but differentiated.

Your job is to give clients your alliance, commitment, and empathy as they go through their process of responding to your retirement. However, you may slip up at times and feel triggered. This is natural and likely to happen. When this occurs, you can return to your own grounding practices to stay centered.

Your goal is also to help clients achieve as much closure as possible, given the time remaining, to fulfill their expectations of care and the objectives of treatment. Whether client-initiated or therapist-driven, endings can offer opportunities for growth and healing. Even in a forced ending, you have the potential to provide clients with a positive first-time experience of a trusted, safe relationship that ends well.

Some therapists in our workshops have said that they won't need to prepare in the way we're describing. They believe that because they do short-term work, follow a specific methodology, or work in a clinic or agency with limited sessions, their clients aren't deeply connected to them. Perhaps you think your clients are functioning well enough that they no longer need you. But those who are seeing you in therapy might feel very differently.

When we did a quick read of chat board discussions centered around the closing of therapy practices, we found statements from anonymous readers like these:

- "My therapist had gone out on maternity leave, and she was due to return to the practice in January. She did not come back to the practice. I felt my fears that she would stay home and leave practice entirely were confirmed. I was devastated."
- "How can I find closure for an abrupt abandonment when this therapist fulfilled a motherly role?"
- "My therapist left her practice with little notice, I miss her. I am in pain, not having a therapist anymore."
- "I would literally want to die if he closed his practice, he means that much to me."
- "If my therapist left with no further contact possible, my heart would break."

As you'll see in the next chapter, which explores client attachment and how attachment styles manifest in endings, your clients may have a much harder time saying goodbye than you expect. To facilitate a full and meaningful ending, you need to create space for them to express their feelings, thoughts, and fantasies about your departure. This will allow them to process and grow from the experience. It's essential to listen receptively and understand how much you mean to your clients.

Staying Secure

Staying internally secure, before and during a stressful ending process with those who depend on you, is an important therapeutic skill—one you may need to practice over time.

Here are nine suggestions that are helpful to calm anxiety, stress, reactivity, or worries (Wehrenberg, 2008). They will promote inner security and enable you to respond with less reactivity or anxiety as you anticipate the process of ending therapy with clients who depend on you, or as you consider leaving an organization where you are involved with teams, colleagues, associates, or students. You may need to use some or all of these to help you feel confident during your ending process:

- **Make a plan:** Staying secure within yourself and offering comfort to yourself can be enhanced by making a solid decision and plan. Being able to remind yourself, *I have a plan and I am following my plan*, can help you stay calm in those moments of indecision when a client or a colleague challenges you on why you are retiring. If you are a person who has always been comfortable waiting to see how things go, who likes to "go with the flow," then planning might feel uncomfortable, but it becomes a life raft in a potentially turbulent emotional sea of changing your life from employed to retired. Allow your desire to go with the flow to apply to other aspects of your retirement if you must. As you follow the plan you have set with each client, and as you stay consistent with your goals, you will be able to set and maintain your boundaries and facilitate your clients' processes. Having a plan for ending helps you to remain predictable, be accountable to yourself and to your clients, and protect your clients' best interests.
- **Identify and utilize friends and colleagues:** Staying secure in oneself does not mean going it alone. People with secure attachment styles utilize their relationships to restore calm in themselves. As you contemplate retirement and plan for it, bring your friends along. Talk to them about your goals and get their feedback. Let them know your decisions and, if you start to waffle once you are in process of saying goodbye to clients, ask them to remind you that you decided this after careful consideration. Furthermore, take advantage to use any supervisor or group you participate in to talk through challenges within yourself.
- **Give your brain a break or sleep on it:** Staying secure might require you to stop thinking about the problem of retiring. There will be times when you may be a bit overwhelmed by the implications and details of the decision. You can let your brain's default mode network help out. Whether you are intentionally thinking over a problem or not, your brain will be actively working to resolve it. You can tap the power of this automatic system in your brain by allowing your mind to wander. Try this: Think about whatever aspect of your retirement decision is troubling you. Then go for a walk without earbuds, or sit and look at water moving or a fire flickering—whatever you do, do *not* try to think about the issue. Returning to the problem later, you will likely find that you have some new

ideas or perhaps some clarity on how to proceed. Just put off the decision for a day and sleep on it. Upon awakening, you may well have a good idea of how to proceed. A good night's sleep makes everything clearer, and courses of action became easier to decide.

- **Block interruptions:** Stress is intensified by the constant demands to pay attention—especially being asked to pay attention to something irrelevant to our task at hand. It is hard to continue feeling secure if you are continuously coping with incoming information unrelated to the moment. It is especially easy to let our devices grab our attention. Responding to the interruptions, we become easily diverted by the sense of urgency that a text or question from a colleague might convey. Confusing urgency with importance, we drop our necessary task, only to have it weigh undone on our minds. Our stress levels rise under those conditions. If you are feeling anxious or stressed as you move toward retirement, try giving yourself some uninterrupted "me time" to do whatever work will allow you the most stress relief without eliminating your "me time" altogether. Such tasks might be work-related, such as finishing discharge summaries, getting the billing done, returning calls, or preparing for a lecture you are to give. Give yourself time to do the tasks that wrapping up a therapy practice will ask of you, turning off your devices to finish reports or complete client billing.
- **Avoid ambiguity:** Anxiety is the natural response to ambiguity. Your clients' anxieties will rise if your retirement plan is ambiguous, and so will yours. Make sure you have done a cost-benefit analysis affirming the benefits of your decision to retire; be fully aware of potential downsides. Once you accept the downsides as reasonable and worth the action to retire, you can feel secure that you are following the right path.
- **Remember that few choices in life are irrevocable:** This is not a sanction to be indecisive, change your mind on a whim, or swing back and forth with your plan. Rather, if after careful consideration you need to redo your cost-benefit analysis with fresh information, you can change your mind about retirement. You can continue working if you must. Just knowing that might help reduce anxiety about making the right choice.

- **Use stress-reducing methods:** Meditation, yoga, walking, and other regular exercise activities bring endless benefits for thinking and staying healthy. For immediate stress, remember to breathe! Take a long, slow inhale, and focus on a long, slow exhale. It does not have to be obvious to anyone else, but this slow breath can give you the equivalent of a pause, like counting to ten and clearing your mind for the moment. If you are in the midst of a challenging moment with a client or coworker, consider saying, "I want to pause a moment to think about my response." Then take that moment. Breathe. You may want to ask God, the universe, or your own mind to offer some helpful words. Then focus on your breath. Chances are that a helpful response will come to you.
- **Stop ruminating:** If you become caught up in rethinking your decision, ask yourself immediately: Is the rumination helping me? Rethinking your decisions about any phase of retirement might be a signal that you need more information. During the process of planning, when you feel confused or overwhelmed, stop often and consider what further information you may need. If you need *more* information, plan how to obtain it. If you are only rehashing things already thought through, your rumination may be a sign of anxiety reflecting momentary insecurity. Go back to your plan, review your written cost-benefit analysis, or ask a good friend to refresh your memory. In the meantime, interrupt the rumination by using self-talk, such as, *I have good reasons. I will think of them in a moment.* Distract yourself for a few minutes: listen to music, read, talk to someone, play a game, or watch a program. Pull yourself out of looping, repetitive thoughts.
- **Add self-acceptance:** Self-acceptance does not mean retirement will always be an easy process. It means knowing this is the right time to let go of the work you love, even if it is hard. If you have been working because you should or ought to (fill in the many reasons you *should* keep working) then staying secure in yourself will be much easier when you identify the impact of should. Those "shoulds" may come in several forms: I *should* keep working as long as I can think, until my spouse retires, or to prove I am still a capable person. The goal is for you to accept that you are worthy and loveable as a retired person. Self-acceptance is necessary to shift from precontemplation into contemplation and beyond.

—*Exercise*—

Staying Secure Inside Myself

This exercise includes the nine suggestions for staying secure internally before and during a stressful ending process. Include one or more ways you can follow each.

Make a plan.

____

____

____

____

Identify and utilize friends and colleagues.

____

____

____

____

Rest your brain or sleep on it.

____

____

____

____

Block interruptions.

____

____

____

____

Avoid ambiguity.

Remember that few choices in life are irrevocable.

Use stress-reducing methods.

Stop ruminating.

Add self-acceptance.

Moving Forward

At this point, you have completed the first of a three-step plan for dealing with forced endings. With a grasp on how you will stay grounded and secure inside yourself during the retirement process, you can move on to the next two steps of the plan to manage ending.

Now let's look deeper at the issues of client attachment and what can surface during a forced ending. In the next chapter, you will see strategies and objectives that can help create a safe, secure ending for you, your clients, your teams, and your staff.

—*Chapter 5*—

Client Attachment in Ending

"Promise me you will not leave the clinic—that you will stay as long as I am in therapy, even if it takes months," a young client pleads with her therapist, who is privately considering retirement before the end of the year. When a client feels connected to a therapist, what happens when the therapist announces the decision to leave? Is it possible to close a case—or an entire caseload— for your own reasons and still ensure a good therapeutic completion for those you treat?

As we discussed in the previous chapter, when a therapist ends treatment due to retirement, it's called a *forced ending*. This means the client has little control over how or when therapy concludes. In this chapter, we'll review the importance of the client-therapist attachment and how it can be impacted during a forced ending, helping you better understand what to expect in the process. Since clients invest significant time, money, and emotional energy in therapy, the announcement of a forced ending can trigger upsetting reactions. These reactions can be challenging for both the client and therapist to navigate effectively.

In the previous chapter, we outlined a three-step plan for handling forced endings, which we'll revisit here. In this chapter, we'll focus on step two: assessing how your clients' attachment styles can influence the process of a forced ending in psychotherapy. Step 3 will be discussed in the next chapter.

Three-Step Plan for Therapist-Initiated Forced Endings

1. Practice staying grounded and secure inside yourself.
2. **Understand client attachment and help clients process their anger, pain, grief, or loss by staying present, responsive, and empathic.**
3. Recognize your own reactions and process in ending.

A Unique Connection

First, let's consider the importance of the connections you have built with your clients. As therapists, we work hard to foster an open and empathic relationship with our clients for a fundamental, clinical reason: The attachment between clients and their therapists is a crucial, necessary element for the effectiveness and positive outcome of therapy.

Whether we see clients in a short-term cognitive model or use longer-term analytic, somatic, or emotive methods, client attachment to the therapist is closely correlated to the purpose, process, and outcome of psychotherapy or counseling.

Early studies found that most therapeutic methods worked equally well, regardless of the approach used, due to an "implicit common factor" in therapy: a strong therapeutic connection between therapist and client (Rosenzweig, 1936). Later research emphasized that even more important is the client's *perception* of that relationship—their sense of alliance with you; this is a key factor in determining positive therapeutic outcomes (Duncan et al., 2010). A client's attachment to the therapist, along with their feelings about the relationship, should be explored and addressed throughout all phases of treatment—including the ending stage. Clients form attachments to their therapists whether therapy is short-term or long-term. These attachments can begin as early as the first hello, sometimes even through an initial email or phone call—often in ways you might not consciously notice or acknowledge. As humans, we are biologically wired to form attachments, and since your clients come to therapy at their most vulnerable states, facing problems they can't resolve alone, their attachment may stem from basic human survival instincts.

Client Reactions When Ending Treatment

The lack of control over the ending of treatment can threaten a client's well-being or mental health, so it's crucial for you, as the therapist, to anticipate and reflect on their needs ahead of time. Even if the course of therapy is short-term and the timeline has been agreed upon, be aware that the attachment bonds, desire for control, and reluctance to end therapy may still persist. Consider the range of potential reactions your clients might experience, regardless of their age, gender, length of treatment, or the modality you use. The goal is to understand your clients' emotional responses and help them navigate their feelings and concerns so you can close your practice in a way that supports both their well-being and your own.

When clients are told that therapy is ending due to the therapist's own needs—such as retirement, illness, or caregiving—they can experience a wide range of emotions, thoughts, and behaviors. Being alert to individual clients' reactions will help you guide their treatment through the rough waters of reactivity and provide positive therapeutic outcomes.

Therapists we surveyed shared stories of notifying clients, only to face reactions like anger, abandonment, rejection, guilt, relief, fear, denial, betrayal, sadness, grief, liberation, and even envy. For example, if a client is bonded to the therapist and fears that leaving will be a sad and painful series of sessions, they may not want to go through the emotional process of ending; instead, they suddenly announce that they are leaving in two weeks. They leave you first, rather than be abandoned. They may tell you that they have already found a "better" therapist, rejecting you rather than being rejected by you.

Another client may react as though being left is a personal affront, sure that you are leaving because you are tired of working with them or don't like them. They might begin to question your commitment to them and receive your retirement as a narcissistic injury. This client may insist that you are kicking them out and cite reasons for this, pointing to something unexplored or unaddressed earlier in the treatment.

A client may also undo previous gains made in therapy and regress to more symptomatic behaviors as a way of expressing their sad and anxious feelings about you ending their treatment. A client may feel unable to go on without you, ask for more sessions in the time that is left, beg you to make an exception and extend treatment, or become unusually clingy with phone calls and texts.

Some clients may immediately go into denial—they insist that ending is fine and your leaving is not a problem for them, despite a history of a substantial therapeutic connection with you. Others may avoid their feelings about the announcement by refusing to talk about it in subsequent sessions, not believing you will really leave them or end their sessions until the time is finally upon them. When this time comes, they may express shock, apparently not remembering that you repeatedly announced your ending date.

Reactions may be subtle. A client may communicate their feelings by reporting dreams or thoughts about a similar ending or loss; when interpreted, these may be able to be claimed as feelings about what is happening between the client and the therapist in the ending process. Whatever the reactions, subtle or blatant, they do not necessarily signal that therapy was unproductive. Regressions based on the stress of ending don't necessarily reflect the course of therapy.

Instead, you can recognize the announcement of a forced ending as an attachment-defining moment—a rupture in the secure and safe bond that was in place. However, with enough time and readiness, this rupture can be processed, worked through, and repaired. Some clients may even feel relief and celebrate the ending, viewing it as a kind of graduation. With adequate preparation for the conclusion of treatment, many clients can have positive experiences when saying goodbye.

With your guidance, they can better understand their own resilience and ability to move on. By taking part in a thoughtful and structured ending process, they can experience appreciation and a mutual sense of goodwill or affection, allowing both therapist and client to part ways with a sense of completion and accomplishment.

While some clients may feel resolved and untroubled by the ending of therapy, it's important to focus on situations that could present challenges for you as a therapist. This will help you prepare for a wide range of responses and reactions.

Client Attachment Styles in Forced Endings

You can help your clients better understand their reactivity by viewing the final stage of therapy through the lens of attachment styles. When clients can identify what might be triggered inside them, they can use their remaining time with the therapist to create a more constructive ending. By reviewing attachment styles and how they manifest during endings, clients gain cognitive insights into the emotional experience of being left or needing to end therapy before they were ready. This understanding can help them feel more in control and bring structure to the process of closure.

Educating your clients about attachment styles—unconscious preverbal relational patterns observed in children and their parents—can shed light on how these early experiences shape how they relate to others throughout their lives. You might even suggest they take one of the many free online attachment style quizzes to help pinpoint which style resonates most with them.

There are four primary attachment styles, and research suggests these early patterns often persist into adulthood. The attachment bonds that may be disrupted in a forced ending are sometimes referred to by therapists as an "attachment crisis" (Power, 2015). The following list is a brief overview of each of the four most common attachment styles—secure, anxious, avoidant, and disorganized—and how clients with these styles might react or become distressed during a forced ending in therapy:

- **Secure attachment:** A *secure attachment* happens when caretakers offer a safe space that allows children to feel seen, safe, and confident that their basic needs will be met. Those who are securely attached got "good enough parenting," and as adults, can rely on the internalized sense of safety and confidence to self-soothe loss, hurt, and minor upsets without mental decompensation. As these children mature, they tend to be resilient, seeing minor setbacks as potential opportunities, and they may welcome the termination of therapy as a chance for outward exploration.
    - **In ending:** A securely attached person may be ready to "graduate" therapy when the therapist retires, with a feeling of being ready for therapy to end. The client may express appropriate emotion to ending treatment, such as feelings of loss, sadness, or some worry about the future, but they can usually review gains made in therapy as a way to end with confidence. The client can be encouraged to reclaim positive attributes that are put on the therapist, like nurturance and kindness, to see how to find these attributes in themselves. They may express missing the therapist but can feel appreciation and recognize the healing that happened as a result of therapy. Many people with this attachment style feel well positioned to move forward without the therapist or needing further therapy when their treatment ends.

    Which of your clients might be best described as having a *secure* attachment style?

- **Anxious or ambivalent attachment:** An *anxious or ambivalent attachment* is created when caretakers are inconsistent or erratic, or the child experiences excessive fear and a lack of basic safety in the home environment. Those who are anxiously attached can't easily trust themselves or others, suffer from panic or other anxiety symptoms, have low self-esteem, and may get easily confused or overwhelmed in the face of close relationships. They are often insecure about how to receive or give love and blame themselves for not being able to connect. They may feel very dependent on the therapist and on the course of therapy, and the fact of ending can be disruptive and frightening.
    - **In ending:** An anxiously attached client may be a hardworking, consistent therapy client, but in the face of a forced ending, they may become needy,

clingy, and insecure. They can regress to earlier symptoms of anxiety and depression or feel suicidal. They might express envy or jealousy that the therapist will leave them for a "better life" in retirement and become angry or critical of the work that has already been done. They may rail at the fact that the therapist is leaving them during their time of greatest need. They may insist on having a referral in place before the therapy comes to an end, and some may go through a roller coaster of emotions as the time of ending nears.

Which of your clients might be best described as having an *anxious* or *ambivalent* attachment style?

- **Avoidant-dismissive attachment:** An *avoidant attachment* is thought to be the result of angry, strict, or distant caretakers who lack consistent nurturing and warmth to create a home environment of safety and security. Those who are avoidantly attached are often trying desperately to get noticed, which evolves into being high achievers or acting out in some form. They can be unemotional and have trouble with the softer skills of nurturing or intimate relationships. Those who are avoidantly attached believe they do better or best alone and gravitate toward independence over a need for connection. They may lack the skills or instinct to be able to bond deeply with others. They tend to be type A, high-control individuals, and while they may appear confident, they often fail at intimate relationships because they can't or don't show vulnerability.
    - **In ending:** An avoidantly attached client may express little or no emotion after the announcement. The therapist may find that the client refuses to explore much about the upcoming termination due to a combination of denial and distancing. These clients may fight for a sense of control by punishing or rejecting the therapist. They may deny that the relationship is important and leave first, before being left. Some may pick arguments with the therapist and create conflict rather than explore underlying softer feelings of sadness, grief, and loss. For the avoidant client, being "abandoned" or "quit on" becomes further evidence that investing in relationships like therapy is unproductive and unnecessary.

Which of your clients might be best described as having an *avoidant-dismissive* attachment style?

- **Disorganized attachment:** A *disorganized attachment*, also known as a fearful style, is often the result of trauma, abuse, or extreme danger present in the home. The source of the child's fear may be the caregivers themselves, with few options for the child to stay safe. A client with disorganized attachment is often confused and unpredictable, unable to determine who or what is safe. Most people with this style can't trust others in relationships; although they may seek closeness, they lack the skills or ability to assess the right people to bond with, and they likely feel very alone. These are clients who present with trauma or other conditions and suffer from significant pain, abandonment, and loss. It may have taken a long time for them to trust their therapist and commit to the process of treatment.
    - **In ending:** A client who has a fearful or disorganized attachment may be unpredictable and extremely distressed with the announcement of a forced ending. They may sabotage the final stage of therapy to deny themselves or their therapist a good ending, expecting that no relationship will ever end well. They may feel or behave aggressively, feel punished or become punishing, or insist that they are helpless in the face of this situation or that future life is hopeless. They take the ending personally and find it difficult to comprehend how the therapist can change the rules of treatment, which they understood would end on their terms and timeline. In extreme cases, they may regress, insist they can't function without the therapist, or threaten suicide or self-harm to hold the therapist closer.

    Which of your clients might be best described as having a *disorganized* or *fearful* attachment style?

Given the complexity of possible reactions, it is important to give yourself and your clients as much advance notice as possible so that you have time to process through these potential triggers. To move forward with the goals and objectives of a good ending, take time to process that ending, whether the therapy contract is for short- or long-term sessions. With this concept of attachment in mind, you can begin to outline your objectives when bringing treatment to an end.

Objectives of a Good Ending

Each client is unique, and we all use different modalities in our work. However, regardless of your approach or the population you serve, we encourage you to set clear objectives *with* your clients for a better ending. Clients need to have a sense of control and a voice in how their final weeks, months, or even years of therapy will progress. By incorporating structure into the process, you can help ensure that the ending feels safe and thoughtfully considered. Allow your clients to understand and appreciate the care you're putting into this final phase of treatment. Depending on the timeframe of the ending, you can clarify what is feasible to focus on and address, helping both you and your clients feel more complete as therapy concludes.

I (Lynn) have always focused on providing good endings, whether it means leaving enough time at the end of a session for my clients to summarize what we've discussed and not feel rushed, or asking them to give me advance notice when they are ready to leave therapy. I make it clear to my clients that with notice, I can guide them through a process and help them end well, even if they're unsure how to structure a good closure. With a forced ending, I would approach it the same way—by putting the same thought, structure, and time into the process. Providing sufficient notice to clients and setting clear objectives for what to focus on in their final months, year, or even two years can help make this a smooth and meaningful conclusion.

—Exercise—

Objectives in Ending

Goals to help your clients feel a sense of completion may include some or all of these objectives (this list is geared to adult clients—please adapt for the age and population of your own caseload). Place a check on the following goals that are important to you and modify or adjust for your situation, methods, or ways of working:

- ❒ **Help the client recognize their early attachment style** to anticipate or identify thoughts, feelings, behaviors, or patterns that may be triggered during the ending phase of therapy.
- ❒ **Review the beginning of treatment** and the presenting problems to reflect on the client's experience of therapy, feelings about the therapeutic relationship, and cognitive and behavioral progress made.
- ❒ **Acknowledge achievements throughout the course of treatment** and consolidate gains. Clarify the focus of therapy going forward, with specific goals that can be accomplished within the remaining time frame. Discuss goals that can be continued after therapy ends without the therapist's support.
- ❒ **Review steps, strategies, methods, and homework** that have helped the client regulate emotions, process and cope with trauma, and reduce anxiety and stress.
- ❒ **Consider existing community resources and support** that can help maintain therapeutic progress and identify additional resources that may be necessary post-therapy.
- ❒ **Help the client reclaim projections** (such as attributes placed onto the therapist) that belong to them, like the ability to listen to themselves, nurture their own needs, and accept deeper feelings and thoughts.

- ❒ **Identify the client's sense of hope and optimism** for both their short-term and long-term future and work with them to create a plan for next steps after therapy ends.
- ❒ **Validate the client's effort, commitment, and investment** throughout therapy.
- ❒ **Provide feedback to the client** about how the therapist felt regarding the work done together, including appreciation for the time and shared experience, and express well wishes for the client's future well-being.
- ❒ **Allow time for the client to give feedback** about the therapy process—what worked, what didn't, what they appreciated, and any wishes for what could have been different.
- ❒ **Express gratitude** for the client's efforts and feedback.
- ❒ **Other:** ____

  ____

  ____

  ____

  ____

Moving Forward

If you'd like to read more about attachment styles in relation to forced endings in therapy, a helpful reference that has informed our thinking is *Forced Endings in Psychotherapy and Psychoanalysis: Attachment and Loss in Retirement* by Anne Power (2015).

In the next chapter, you will see the other side of the attachment coin—the reactivity or emotional dysregulation that can occur in the therapist's own process during a forced ending. Learn more about the issues that may get triggered from your own history of endings and how to resolve them to help your clients end well.

—Chapter 6—

The Therapist's Ending Process

Sonia is a seventy-three-year-old licensed professional counselor. She cried a bit while talking about her upcoming plan to close her practice by the end of the year. "I just am so torn up about this decision," she said. "I see teenage girls with eating disorders. I feel like I am abandoning them. It wasn't their choice for me to disrupt treatment. I am retiring for my own selfish reasons. These girls are more to me than just clients—they are more like my daughters. How can I leave them? I can't sleep. I am grieving, big time."

Sonia feels heartbroken to leave her teenage clients. At face value, this sadness could make sense because all of us tend to invest in our therapy clients. Week after week, month after month, we listen to and hold our clients' lives and stories in our awareness. But Sonia's upset goes beyond what we might consider the normal feelings of closing a caseload. She can't sleep. She cries daily, and she thinks of them as daughters. Her grief conveys something deeper in her own history, beyond her professional role.

Later, in peer supervision, Sonia raises her concerns about retiring and leaving her young clients. She links her sadness to an issue in her personal history. Her younger sister died by suicide as a teenager while Sonia was away at college. Sonia felt guilty for years and wondered if she could have prevented this if she had stayed home instead of going away.

Sonia believed this issue was resolved long ago in her own therapy, but as her retirement draws near, it has resurfaced. She feels as though she is abandoning the vulnerable teenagers on her caseload, much like she did with her sister. It's no wonder she feels so bereft and is grieving. With this new awareness, Sonia decides to seek additional support through supervision with a consulting therapist and more individual therapy sessions to address the issue. She understands that she cannot provide a secure and safe ending for her clients unless she feels at peace and guilt-free about her retirement plans.

Our emotional responses as we close our cases can often surprise us. In many ways, our own therapy is never truly complete. As new circumstances arise, old issues can resurface, calling for renewed reflection and growth. Retirement, in particular, presents its own set of challenges. The more we stay attuned to our emotional responses, the better equipped we will be to navigate the process of closure.

Understanding Your Reactions in Ending

The third goal in the Three-Step Plan for Forced Endings is to recognize and stay attuned to your emotional reactions, particularly any countertransference, as you end therapy with clients. This is often the most difficult and complex of the three steps. In this chapter, we offer a framework to help you understand and address any triggers, unconscious issues, or concerns that may arise as you navigate the ending process.

As a reminder, we are now focusing on the final step of the three-step plan.

Three-Step Plan for Therapist-Initiated Forced Endings

1. Practice staying grounded and secure inside yourself.
2. Understand client attachment and help clients process their anger, pain, grief, or loss by staying present, responsive, and empathic.
3. **Recognize your own reactions and process in ending.**

Based on the therapists we surveyed and interviewed, coping with some reactivity or countertransference during the process of ending your caseload and career is not uncommon.

June is set to retire in six months and has informed all of her clients about this—except for one. This particular client is a woman close to June's age, one of her first clients. Over time, June has helped her through many changes and has developed a strong sense of liking and respect for her. While June has informed all her other clients about her upcoming retirement, she delays telling this particular one, claiming that she simply can't bring herself to announce her departure. Instead, she avoids it, and in her notes, she writes, *Have not notified this client, can't handle ending with her.* This represents a form of denial on the therapist's part. June knows she must inform the client yet continues to put it off, session after session, despite understanding that it is unfair to the client.

Outside of therapy sessions, June has a fantasy—one she keeps to herself but often thinks about: What if she and this client could transition from therapy to friendship? That way, she wouldn't have to let go of the relationship. In this daydream, June avoids the pain and loss of saying goodbye. Fortunately, she brings this fantasy into a consultation session with a fellow therapist, who helps her explore how to separate her own feelings of loss and longing. The consulting therapist encourages June to view her fantasy as an indication of a deeper concern. June begins to recognize that she is grieving, but she also admits that she has relied on her clients to fill a void in her life, realizing that she lacks real friendships outside of her work.

With this awareness, June takes the step to inform her client promptly about her impending retirement. She feels both sad and relieved.

Most of us can concede that we have feelings and thoughts about our clients, both in and out of sessions. Thinking about our cases is natural and part of the human experience. We react to what happens around us and are impacted by those around us. Intuition, inklings, or subtle reactions can add to our insight as we try to understand and empathize with our clients.

When reactivity goes beyond a subtle response and becomes an expression of unconscious issues, or when it drives behaviors that deviate from your usual practices, it becomes your responsibility to ensure that your personal history or anxiety does not interfere with your client's ability to end therapy well. Most therapists receive training and support to identify and manage their reactions, behaviors, and biases, especially when these become obstacles to the goals of therapy. If you're feeling conflicted about your retirement deadline, your caseload, how to transition your responsibilities, or the pressure of a retirement to-do list, your reactivity can be triggered unconsciously and may become problematic.

Here are some additional examples of unconscious reactions that would need to be addressed or managed by a therapist:

- A retiring therapist whose office lease is coming due feels pressured and pushes a client to accept a referral for further treatment that is not best for the client or what the client says she wants.
- A therapist, ambivalent about retiring, keeps changing the date of her practice closing. Her clients can't plan to find other treatment options since there is no clear plan for when their treatment with her will end. In session, clients begin to express increasing anxiety and uncertainty about the future of their ongoing treatment; the therapist is unable to soothe them since she is so anxious herself. In supervision, the therapist is cautioned that she seems to have created a situation of *mirroring*: By not dealing with her own anxiety about leaving, she has passed it on to her clients, who now reflect it back to her.
- A mental health clinic director resents being told to retire due to his age and begins to sabotage the transfer of information. He loses files, erases data, and forgets to attend meetings, making it hard for his successor to start the job well. When spoken to about this, he feels defensive and unappreciated.
- A therapist who is retiring sooner than expected due to her own health concerns begins to self-disclose too much detail about her illness. She discloses more in each session, generating sympathy from her clients to buffer herself and avoid dealing with their upset at the disruption of treatment. Her clients can't explore a full range of feelings since they feel concerned for their therapist's health. Her disclosure and their worry prevent them from a more complete ending.
- A therapist decides to partially retire, letting go of the "more-involved" clients—those who have complex mental health needs and require adjunct service—while holding on to the few clients whose diagnoses are less demanding. He tells the first group of clients that he is retiring but says nothing to the smaller group of clients he will continue seeing. He knows this conflicts with his profession's ethical code of treating clients equally and nonjudgmentally, but he justifies his behavior by saying he is exhausted.

Monitoring Yourself

The way through reactivity or countertransference is to use self-awareness, and when needed, seek outside professional support. Take time to monitor your own thoughts, feelings, and reactions as they occur in each client case. Remember, having emotions about client endings is normal, but must be addressed if it interferes with sessions, meetings, or managerial responsibilities. It helps to review your personal experience with endings (see chapter 5) and note what may get triggered from your own history as you make plans to retire. Bring in trusted peers and supervisors to help you make sense of any reactivity and resolve to monitor yourself during this process.

—Exercise—

Self-Monitoring Checklist

As you move forward with your retirement planning—including notifying clients—monitor your emotions, thoughts, and behaviors. Place a check next to the following emotions you are feeling or behaviors you have noticed:

- ❒ Shame that you are secretly relieved, glad to finally be rid of a difficult caseload
- ❒ Longing to stop giving so much of yourself and your time to clients; feeling selfish for wanting to be free
- ❒ Grieving; using language about death, loss, life being over; sensing depression and despair that this part of your career is at an end
- ❒ Missing clients already, even before you have closed your practice
- ❒ Rushing sessions; feeling detached, uninterested, or unmoved during sessions, as though you are emotionally already gone
- ❒ Guilt, feeling like you are hurting clients when you make plans to take care of yourself
- ❒ Other: ______________________________

____

____

____

____

RETIREMENT JOURNAL

Tracking Your Process

Monitor your feelings and actions regarding retirement by reflecting on the following prompts in your retirement journal:

- As you think about leaving your clients and your career, what feelings are you having?
- What clients, projects, or situations feel the most difficult to let go of?
- What clients, projects, or situations feel the easiest to let go of?
- How might these feelings be changing your daily behavior, mood, or competence?
- How have these feelings and behaviors been affecting your work or time away from work?

Attachment Issues for the Therapist When Retiring

We have discussed how a forced ending can cause a possible attachment crisis for the client (chapter 5), but it can also trigger an attachment issue for the therapist. Similar to what your clients may experience in ending therapy based on their early attachment styles, therapists can feel distress that is influenced by their own attachment styles. If you know your attachment style and can anticipate what may occur with clients as you initiate a forced ending to retire from your work, it can help you feel more prepared.

Review again the four most common attachment styles and see if you recognize your own. Then read what you may need to expect when ending with clients:

- **Secure attachment:** Therapists with secure attachment to themselves, their work, and their professional roles would be able to stay calm, empathic, and resourceful in the midst of client distress, anger, blaming, or other defensiveness. The securely attached therapist would be nonreactive when these responses occur and make space in sessions to help the client refocus on the goals of the ending process. The therapist would not deny the existence of the complexity of the ending, and instead would allow for the time and attention it takes to say goodbye. The therapist would structure the last stages of therapy to help the client have a good ending, even if it meant not completing all the previous objectives of therapy.

- **In ending:** This therapist focuses on the objectives of a good ending: reviewing client gains, feedback, and validation for all the client has accomplished and appreciating their commitment to therapy. The therapist can recognize client attachment issues in ending and complement these—for example, by staying calm in the face of anger, being compassionate if the client is grieving, or allowing for client longings to remain working together. The therapist can recognize and accept the frustration of what was not completed in therapy and express appropriate regret. They can receive the gratitude of the client without deflecting or discounting the expressions of appreciation.

Do you have a *secure* attachment style, and if so, does this describe what you might anticipate in ending?

- **Anxious or ambivalent attachment:** If a therapist has an anxious attachment style, retirement may provoke feelings of worry and fear about what will happen to their clients when therapy ends. In worst cases, therapists may actively project these worries and fears onto their clients, losing the ability to accurately assess their level of vulnerability or strength. If, due to their own anxious attachment, therapists are convinced that their clients can't endure without them, they may extend their leaving date indefinitely. Therapists may need continual reassurance that they are entitled to retire—a way to cope with guilt and regret—and assistance in believing that their clients can survive (or even thrive) without them.
  - **In ending:** This therapist may want to make special exceptions to end with some clients but continue with others whom they deem helpless to function without them. The therapist may infantilize their clients, become enmeshed with them, or even see themselves as irreplaceable. Even after closing cases, an anxious therapist may dream and wonder about the lives of clients, fantasizing about reconnecting or finding them on social media "just to see how they are doing." If therapists act on these longings, they may be in an ethical breach, given their licensure. Not letting go may undermine the value of allowing clients to graduate, stand on their own, find other treatment or support options, and connect with a new therapist.

Do you have an *anxious* or *ambivalent* attachment style, and if so, does this describe what you might anticipate in ending?

- **Avoidant-dismissive attachment:** Therapists with an avoidant attachment style may feel some guilt about retirement, but generally, they want to get it over with and move on. They can usually hold boundaries well around the policies of a forced ending—announcing it clearly, setting up a firm deadline for stopping, and being clear about what resources they will or will not provide for clients. But in times of stress or reactivity, they may lack the patience and empathy to allow the loss and grief of clients to play out and resolve. Some therapists with this attachment style are unfamiliar with processing strong or complicated emotions. They prefer to focus on actions, shifting from discussions of feelings to the pragmatic steps of ending a case.

  - **In ending:** This therapist may begin to distance and withdraw from clients even before the retirement announcement is made. They may find it difficult to allow the full spectrum of emotions to play out in the ending process with their clients. Some who do short-term therapy may believe a drawn-out ending process is not necessary, given the brief nature of treatment, and rush past the full unfolding or complete exploration of their clients' losses. Some therapists naturally do less processing in a session, utilizing more behavioral methods. These therapists need to watch for their own irritation or frustration when clients want to express feelings including envy, abandonment, upset, or anxiety about the end of treatment.

  Do you have an *avoidant-dismissive* attachment style, and if so, does this describe what you might anticipate in ending?

- **Disorganized attachment:** Therapists with this attachment style have often worked hard to regulate their emotions and understand the roots of their own trauma. However, they are still vulnerable to being triggered given the attachment crisis that a forced ending may create in their clients. In their reactivity, it is often difficult for them to set a firm and agreed-upon ending date. Those with this attachment style have their own issues with rejection, abandonment, and distancing, so creating this condition in their clients may be especially troubling and upsetting. They often feel a lot of guilt about retiring.

  - **In ending:** These therapists may make errors—forgetting sessions, stepping over ethical boundaries, self-disclosing too much in the explanation for ending—unintentionally putting their own needs first in the process. They may waver and feel that their clients can't be asked to function without them. Their own distress at ending dominates their ability to stay focused on their clients' needs. They have trouble individuating their own needs and holding firm to their decision to end their cases. They may find themselves teary in sessions and beset with somatic distress outside of their work. In extreme cases, they may slide into a depression or mental health crisis in reaction to the difficult process of closing their caseload. Therapists who find themselves decompensating to this level need the support of therapy or supervision to keep their own issues separate from those of their clients.

Do you have a *disorganized-fearful* attachment style, and if so, does this describe what you might anticipate in ending?

Therapist Guilt

When we spoke with therapists who were in the process of retirement and closing their caseload, the most common theme they expressed was a struggle with guilt.

One therapist explained it this way: "One of my clients was talking about breakup guilt after he left his girlfriend. I realized that I am having breakup guilt, too—not just because I am ready to leave my clients and retire, but also because I am leaving my colleagues who are dear to me and leaving the profession that has been central to my identity. I have attached deeply to all of this for decades and really loved all the parts of my work; it feels just like a romantic breakup. I find myself feeling guilty and sorry, like I need to apologize, but I am not sure to whom? Maybe to myself?"

Guilt can be a very uncomfortable but also useful emotion—at its best, it provokes responsibility and is part of our moral compass. Why does guilt occur for a therapist who is retiring? We hear these three reasons:

1. **Guilt about causing harm:** Because therapists are uncertain about the right way to retire, they worry that their decisions may inadvertently cause harm to others.
2. **Guilt about betraying values**: Therapists struggle to justify putting themselves first in retirement, feeling as though they are going against their ethical responsibilities.
3. **Existential guilt:** At a time when the world needs therapy more than ever, therapists feel guilty for no longer contributing the help they once could.

Your feelings of guilt may be a combination of more than one of these types. Your job is to recognize what is occurring, determine if it is reasonable, try to understand its source, and, if necessary, correct for it.

—Exercise—

Monitoring Therapist Guilt

Note which of the following strategies you might use to monitor and address any feelings of guilt that are obstacles to your retirement:

- ❒ **Work through excessive or irregular feelings** before announcing your retirement, addressing any personal issues that may arise
- ❒ **Pay attention to both obvious and subtle signals of countertransference**, such as perseveration, fantasies, or recurrent thoughts or dreams about clients and their process of ending therapy
- ❒ **Stay open to exploring difficult personal topics** outside of client sessions that retirement may trigger, such as death anxiety, illness, mortality, abandonment, or loneliness
- ❒ **Seek support** through your own therapy, peer supervision, professional supervision, reading, workshops, or other resources to help you stay grounded, aware, and resourceful as you recognize and work through any reactivity
- ❒ **Review and practice the suggestions from chapter 4** that help therapists feel calmer and more secure when terminating or closing cases

Moving Forward

You have completed the contemplation stage for the Readiness for Retirement Model (chapters 4–6), exploring why endings in therapy are difficult, reviewing client attachment styles and possible issues, and assessing your own attachment style and process when ending. By using your retirement journal and the many exercises provided, you have more tools to help you structure constructive and compassionate endings for those who depend on your services.

Now, it's time to enter stage III of the Readiness for Retirement Model: preparation. We provide you with a full exploration of logistics and how-tos, including a ten-step retirement guide, directions on how to prepare for the financial aspects of retirement, and many clear action steps to take. The next chapter will show you how to create a pragmatic, strategic retirement plan.

Stage III

Preparation: The Logistics of Letting Go

The first two stages of the workbook focused on getting clarity on when and why to consider retirement. Now we move on to the *how*. In the chapters of this third stage of getting ready for retirement, we help you become better informed. It's time to examine the logistics and steps to create a customized retirement plan. You may not need to create and enact a retirement plan today, but once you have it in place, you can feel secure and confident about what happens tomorrow.

Instead of asking you to conduct the research and consultation needed to develop a strong retirement plan, we've done it for you here. First, we provide a ten-step guide that covers all the essential practical steps for ending your practice with confidence and care. Then, we help you transition away from the nonclinical roles of business ownership, leadership, and team management while recognizing and valuing the full range of skills you've employed. Additionally, we take a comprehensive look at the role of money in retirement planning, offering solid ideas and resources to help you prepare for both your wants and your needs.

—Chapter 7—

Your Retirement Plan

Do you need a retirement plan right now? Some of you are likely in the precontemplation stage, still happily working and many years away from deciding to stop. Others are in contemplation, thinking seriously about the complications of ending a caseload. Or you may be in preparation, feeling the pressure of an imminent retirement and trying to get organized. Retirement for a therapist can be either a deliberate transition or an unexpected closure. Regardless of when or how you close your practice, having a well-thought-out retirement plan sooner rather than later, can ensure you navigate the process with clarity and confidence.

Unfortunately, many therapists are unsure how to prepare for the closure of their practice. For example, each type of therapist license and location comes with its own set of requirements. Ethical guidelines for maintaining your licensure while closing your practice must be researched, as well as procedures for exiting insurance or EAP contracts without risking legal issues. Closing down your practice can quickly become a job in itself.

To make things easier for you, this chapter focuses on the logistics—the "how-tos"—of ending your practice and leaving your clinical seat. The information provided will give you the foundation to craft your own clear and customized plan. You may need to use it immediately, or you might put it away for years. Regardless of your future plans, having a retirement plan in place ensures a calmer, more secure future.

We provide a no-nonsense guide that includes ten essential steps for closing down. There is no one-size-fits-all plan, so we encourage you to modify the steps to develop the approach that works best for you. We have tried to design the guide to be comprehensive and applicable to most professional therapy licensures. Since licensures and ethical codes vary by therapist type and state, research your specific licensure and state regulations after reviewing this chapter to ensure that you have customized your plan as necessary.

The Ten-Step Retirement Guide

1. Make a retirement timeline, use a calendar, and have a corresponding budget for your plan.
2. Clarify your licensure's ethical codes about ending your practice.
3. Review contracts to alert insurance panels, landlords, licensing boards, and professional associations in a timely manner.
4. Consider getting "tail" malpractice coverage.
5. Compose a message and determine the timing for notifying existing, past, or potential clients.
6. Find referrals for existing clients who need continued care.
7. Conclude your business operation and notify permitting, administrative, accounting, business, and clinical affiliations, as well as any parties with whom you've made legal or financial agreements.
8. Discontinue your marketing efforts, advertising, website, voicemail, online directory listings, and professional social media accounts.
9. Know how to store and ultimately destroy records, documentation, and files.
10. Understand the value of having a professional will in the case you are unable to continue your clinical practice due to your death, illness, or other incapacity.

1. Make a retirement timeline, use a calendar, and have a corresponding budget for your plan.

How much time will you have to end your practice? Do you have a month, a year, five years? Therapists we surveyed said on average that they needed a year minimum to complete their plans and checklists. Some took longer, especially when they had ongoing long-term therapy clients who needed more than a year to complete their work or to transfer to other providers. Whether you have a month or five years to plan, first use a calendar and write out a timeline so you can see what needs to happen in each of the ten steps of the retirement guide.

Add specific dates for the estimated start and completion of each task. Start with the big picture: What is the result? What does practice closure look like at the end of the year? Write it all down. Now back up. What do your findings mean: What will you see or do in nine months, six months, and three months? Work backward to anticipate the time, effort, and expense that you will encounter month by month, until you get to the present day.

Keep a list of your questions. Since therapists operate in different locales under a variety of business permits, professional licensures, and codes of ethics, some of your timeline entries will be things you don't yet know. The time you need to find information still needs to be on your calendar.

Some tasks may repeat on your calendar each month (e.g., finding referrals for clients), while others can be crossed off the list once they are completed (e.g., notifying your professional associations of the date of your retirement.) Some items on your timeline will be specific (e.g., giving a landlord a six-month advance notice of lease termination), while other items may be rough estimates (e.g., one to three months to sort through documents as time allows, determining what to retain and what to destroy.)

Save your notes as you do your research. Retirement requires clinical, professional, ethical, and, at times, legal actions, and should any of your decisions be questioned in the future by clients, insurers, or licensing boards, you want to have good notes and documentation of what you did and why.

Make space for budgeting so you can add the costs associated with each task. For example, if you need to move your office furniture out of a leased office within three months, what will you budget to set up storage and hire a moving company? If you need to dissolve your business entity in nine months, how many times do you need to consult with your accountant or talk to a lawyer, and what will that cost? Just as opening a practice entails some costs, so does ending one.

ACTION STEP: Begin planning your timeline.

____

____

____

____

____

____

—*Exercise*—

Retirement Timeline

In this exercise, you will create a timeline for the tasks you must complete by retirement. Itemize the steps you will need to take, month by month, for a calendar year, including an estimated budget for each step. It will be most helpful to begin with the steps in the Ten-Step Retirement Guide as a guide, but you may add any other tasks you feel may be necessary. An example is included for you first.

The Ten-Step Retirement Guide

1. Make a retirement timeline, use a calendar, and have a corresponding budget for your plan.
2. Clarify your licensure's ethical codes about ending your practice.
3. Review contracts to alert insurance panels, landlords, licensing boards, and professional associations in a timely manner.
4. Consider getting "tail" malpractice coverage.
5. Compose a message and determine the timing for notifying existing, past, or potential clients.
6. Find referrals for existing clients who need continued care.
7. Conclude your business operation and notify permitting, administrative, accounting, business, and clinical affiliations, as well as any parties with whom you've made legal or financial agreements.
8. Discontinue your marketing efforts, advertising, website, voicemail, online directory listings, and professional social media accounts.
9. Know how to store and ultimately destroy records, documentation, and files.
10. Understand the value of having a professional will in case you are unable to continue your clinical practice due to your death, illness, or other incapacity.

Retirement Timeline Example

Category	Month 1	Month 2	Month 3	Month 4	Month 5	Month 6
Planning	❒ Make retirement timeline ❒ Review ethical considerations	❒ Get "tail" malpractice coverage				
Notification		❒ Review contracts ❒ Compose client notifications	❒ Notify clients ❒ Find referrals			
Administration Closure		❒ Create professional will	❒ Notify insurance ❒ Notify licensing	❒ Notify professional associations		
Business Closure					❒ Conclude operations ❒ Notify financial lenders	❒ Discontinue marketing ❒ Remove online presence
Final Steps						❒ Records storage
Total Estimated Costs	$ ________	$ ________	$ ________	$ ________	$ ________	$ ________

Retirement Timeline (Months 1–6)

Category	Month 1	Month 2	Month 3	Month 4	Month 5	Month 6
Planning						
Notification						
Administration Closure						
Business Closure						
Final Steps						
Total Estimated Costs	$ ________	$ ________	$ ________	$ ________	$ ________	$ ________

Retirement Timeline (Months 7–12)

Category	Month 7	Month 8	Month 9	Month 10	Month 11	Month 12
Planning						
Notification						
Administration Closure						
Business Closure						
Final Steps						
Total Estimated Costs	$ ______	$ ______	$ ______	$ ______	$ ______	$ ______

2. Clarify your licensure's ethical codes about ending your practice.

As long as you are licensed, you must adhere to any and all ethical requirements of that license. Even if you plan to retire your professional license at some point, a failure to follow the ethical codes when you retire can make you vulnerable to malpractice lawsuits or insurance clawbacks (when insurance companies take payments back from providers due to incorrect behavior).

No one ethical code applies to all licensed therapists. Ethical codes vary license to license and state to state. A comparison composed by Griffin (2010) among a variety of licensures—marriage and family therapists, clinical social workers, and counselors and psychologists—found that standards varied widely in ethical codes regarding issues common in retirement, such as treatment disruption, record storage, license renewal, and the need to make referrals.

Most ethical codes have an overriding concern to avoid abandoning clients without giving them appropriate notice and to provide responsible options for continued care when needed (Barnett & Coffman, 2015). This means that once you have a date for your practice closing, you will want to notify clients earlier, rather than later, to allow all existing clients to be a part of the ending phase of their therapy. Communicate your intention to end therapy with the same level of care and professionalism that you have brought to all other phases of their treatment. Encourage clients to express and process their thoughts and feelings; elicit a set of termination objectives, review resources for continued treatment, and help them look at community-based options for support. Demonstrate and document your thinking, actions, and sensitivity toward helping your clients end as well as possible.

Here are the general guidelines across ethical codes that we can recommend:

- Give clients sufficient clear notice, verbally and in writing.
- Plan with clients for the end of their treatment.
- Openly discuss with your clients your plans for bringing sessions to an end in order to understand their ongoing treatment needs, their goals to complete treatment to their satisfaction, and their concerns about ending.
- Allow enough time for clients to locate and contact other resources or providers for continued care.

- Do not insist that clients must continue treatment or that they accept your referral recommendations. Make recommendations and suggestions and then allow them to make the final decision about further treatment.
- Consult with colleagues or supervisors regarding any at-risk clients who may be negatively impacted by your retirement.
- Document any and all discussions, consultations, and actions you take regarding your practice ending, client concerns, or at-risk client referrals.

ACTION STEP: Make a list of all the actions you need to take to ethically end your practice.

3. Review contracts to alert insurance panels, landlords, licensing boards, and professional associations in a timely manner.

While managing a practice, there are many contracts, permits, and agreements that you operate under. All of these need to be reviewed and assessed as you close things down.

For example, after you retire, do you want to hold onto your license? There is value in keeping your license—once it is surrendered, you can't renew it without a series of difficult reactivating steps. Most therapists we interviewed decided to keep their license active for at least one year after closing their office door. Some told us that in retirement, they decided to engage in community volunteer work, run an occasional supervision group, teach a course, or accept a part-time job; maintaining their license was beneficial for these endeavors. It gave them standing in this phase of retirement. One therapist who retired but did not surrender her license said, "Therapy is a lifetime profession, and I am still alive."

Those who decided differently and let their license lapse often spoke of a sense of relief. They were convinced that they no longer wanted to work in any therapeutic endeavor. Retirement for them was time for relaxation, travel, family, or fun—not more work.

Start early on this step: Contact your licensing board to understand your options and the procedures to follow. Some states allow a category of "retired" or "inactive" for renewal, to allow you to stay licensed but not actually in practice. You are made aware when your license renews, so make sure that you have the requisite continuing education credits in place if you are going to maintain it, even after you officially retire.

Research and assess your existing insurance contractual agreements. If you are an insurance provider, how much time does the insurance company require before you can be removed from the provider panel? What is the process for exit? At a minimum, most insurance companies require written notice, but some require further steps. Read the contract carefully to understand their conditions. Make sure to follow their requirements exactly when terminating with existing insurance-based clients. Fulfill all your contractual obligations. An insurance contract is a legal document, and you must follow what you have promised or you can be open to a lawsuit. Some therapists have found that unpaneling can be a lengthy and complicated process, so make sure that you give yourself the needed time to do this well.

The same advice applies to any other contracts you have signed with landlords, group practice owners, training companies, EAPs, organizations that employ you, or those to whom you pay membership for services. Concluding your membership with professional associations or training organizations can be an emotional experience, so again, give yourself time to take action and then process any feelings or thoughts.

One therapist said that when retiring, her attachment was not only to the profession in general and to her clients, but also to the years of volunteer work she had spent as a part of several training and professional associations: "I attended endless hours of workshops, sat on boards, and volunteered for many, many years to further the methods and support the professional associations that were part of my practice. Fellow board members and training partners became my close friends and are my dear collegial peers. Leaving this part of my professional life was sad and emotional. I was ready to retire my clinical work but didn't think through how many peer relationships would end or fade over time as I said goodbye."

ACTION STEP: Make a list of all ongoing contracts and memberships from which you'll need to begin your exit.

4. Consider getting "tail" malpractice coverage.

Let's imagine that at the same time you retire, you stop your malpractice or liability insurance. But six months later, a disgruntled former client decides to bring you before the licensing board and claims that she was harmed during her time in therapy with you. Your malpractice insurance has since lapsed. The costs of hiring a lawyer and possible damages loom ahead. What are you going to do?

Some policies called *occurrence policies* will cover any situation or incident that occurred when the policy was in place; if you have this kind of insurance, you are still covered for the allegation. However, occurrence policies are rare. Most malpractice policies are *claims-made policies*, a less expensive type that provides less coverage for the therapist. Claims-made policies stop when the insurance contract is over, and future incidents are not covered. If you have one of these, your insurance will not cover any claim made post-retirement.

Research your malpractice insurance before you retire. See if your existing malpractice insurance can be extended once you close your office, with the option of an extended reporting period, also known as *tail malpractice coverage*. This is an add-on to an existing insurance plan that protects you for a period ranging from a year to an unlimited time of your choosing after your practice ends. Tail coverage allows you to report claims against your practice after the policy has been canceled for incidents that occurred while you were covered. You can purchase this coverage at the time of retirement or before, often from your existing malpractice insurer.

Many companies offer various tail packages ranging from a few years to a lifetime. One concern about purchasing tail insurance is the cost, which may be up to three times the cost of your normal malpractice insurance policy. The premiums of tail malpractice insurance are tax deductible as a business expense.

Do you need this coverage? It depends on what kind of insurance you currently have, the nature of your clientele and practice and your retirement plan. One user explains his decision on the Reddit message board r/therapists: "I've been in practice for thirty-five years as a psychologist. No retirement plans in sight for me. But when I do taper my practice and eventually hang it up I will likely purchase a 'tail' for the rest of my life. This is the term for insurance that is retrospective, covering acts in the past. My current policy has a tail which extends back to when I first was licensed—1989—and I'll look into maintaining that tail indefinitely to protect me from a complaint which could conceivably arise from my past practice" (reddit_rabbit507, 2024).

ACTION STEP: Research the details of your current malpractice insurance. If needed, purchase tail coverage.

5. Compose a message and determine the timing for notifying existing, past, or potential clients.

Questions about how and when to announce your retirement and notify your clients were one of the biggest concerns for all the therapists we talked to in writing this book. What should you disclose or not disclose to clients about your decision to retire? When and how far in advance should you tell clients? What is the difference between giving clients time to prepare for the end of treatment versus disrupting their remaining therapy sessions?

The process of notification will vary for each therapist and each individual client based on the issues and impact that your retirement will have. These are sensitive topics, and you need to consider the possible impact on your clients. (If needed, review chapters 4–6, where we provided ways to anticipate what your clients may need from you in ending. We also offered a list of goals and objectives when ending therapy to help you to shape the time remaining for clients to complete their treatment well.)

Although each client you are seeing currently may need a customized process of ending treatment, we recommend that you develop a basic procedure for your notification so that it is consistent and professional. Having a defined process for how you announce your retirement allows you to feel more responsible and predictable during what may be an emotional task. It ensures that all of your clients will be treated equitably and learn about your retirement at the same time.

Are you planning to notify clients during a session? We recommend that after your normal hello or check-in, you begin the session with the news of your forthcoming retirement. Notifying the client at the front end of the session gives them time to respond while still in the session and allows for their initial reactions to happen with you present. (Stay tuned for samples of verbal and written scripts for client notification).

Some therapists may get nervous about the news they are to deliver and leave the announcement until the end of the session as the client is ready to walk out the door. It might relieve your anxiety to be able to convey the news after the session is almost over, but it won't benefit your clients. These "door-closing" communications mean that clients will leave the office with the news unprocessed, forced to deal with questions and feelings on their own.

The best script for your announcement will be clear and direct, disclosing as little as possible in terms of your reasons for closing the practice. Give your clients a chance to fully express and process their own feelings about the news without being short-circuited by their concerns or worries about you, their therapist. Don't muddy the notification with a long explanation about why you are doing this or try to rationalize all the reasons you might have. Instead, treat the announcement as a piece of critical information that needs to be shared simply and plainly. Then give your clients time and space, during the immediate session and in future ones, to have their own authentic responses free of your guilt, regret, upset, or worry.

If the therapist runs groups, all group members should be told at the same time; if the therapist has clients who overlap and know each other, it is preferable that everyone in the caseload gets to hear the news from the therapist herself at the same time, rather than be told by others.

While it is not always advisable for a therapist to attempt to notify all former or inactive clients, there may be inactive clients who come for sessions occasionally or cycle in and out of therapy; you will also need to let them know about the planned closure of the practice, either over the phone or via a letter or email (Griffin, 2010).

A simple verbal script for existing clients might sound something like the following:

> *"I have some news to share with you. As of* [insert date], *I will be retiring and closing my practice. I will work with you to make sure that this ending of therapy can be as positive and complete for you as possible. I will give you more information in future sessions about how we can make this next phase of our work both worthwhile and therapeutic. But today, I want to listen and hear your thoughts and feelings about this."*

A written notification might look something like the following:

> *As of* [insert date], *I will be retiring and closing my practice. I am available to meet with you to answer questions, suggest referrals, and discuss how the process of ending our work will proceed. I will do my best to have the final phase of our work together be as positive and therapeutic for you as possible.*

For clients who are inactive but still occasionally return for sessions, a written notification might look like the following:

> *As of* [insert date], *I will be retiring and closing my practice. I know that we are not meeting on an active basis, but I wanted you to hear this news from me. I am available to meet with you to suggest referrals or to schedule a final session to consolidate the results of our work together.*

The recommended scripts intentionally do not disclose your reasons or rationale for retirement. They do not overpromise results of how the ending will play out or try to sugarcoat or bypass what may be a very difficult time for clients. Instead, they offer your clients the basic information of your retirement and then suggest, as with other topics in therapy, that the focus is on them, not you.

While short-term therapy clients may need only four weeks to ninety days of notice, longer-term ongoing therapy clients may need up to a year of advance notice in order to end well and complete the objectives of their treatment with you. Decide when you will stop accepting new clients. One therapist said that in her opinion, trauma work takes years to complete, so knowing that her retirement date was two years in the future, she decided to stop accepting new clients who needed to work on a history of trauma. You will need to decide on the timing and whether to alert past clients who are inactive but still reach out to you occasionally.

We know that each therapist works differently, and ultimately, you need to rely on your own philosophy, methods, training, and policies. For example, if you are ill or visibly impaired, you may decide that it benefits your clients to know that your practice is ending in an attempt to cope with prior or ongoing illness. Using the process of notification that we have outlined, we hope that the ending phase of therapy can be a holding or contained space for your clients to experience more insight, learning, self-care, and awareness as they complete their work with you.

ACTION STEP: Write or brainstorm ideas for scripts or notifications of announcing to clients your retirement, also considering how you may need to personalize them.

6. Find referrals for existing clients who need continued care.

Not all therapists feel similarly responsible or required to make referrals for clients when they retire. While many therapists feel strongly that referrals for continued care are part of their ethical responsibility, others believe just as strongly that they infantilize clients or remove their agency to make choices for themselves. How does your philosophy and training as a therapist regard transferring clients at the point of the therapist retiring? What are the ethical codes under which you practice? Remember, ethical codes vary license to license and state to state. Review the codes you operate under to see what they say about the need to make or find referrals when the existing therapist is unable to provide treatment.

To explain the variety of how therapists handle providing referrals when ending with clients, we have provided different options from therapists we surveyed who:

- Provided three options for referrals
- Provided no options for referrals
- Screened all potential referrals
- Had no contact with the referrals they suggested
- Facilitated client transfer with files and other documentation
- Provided no written paperwork to transfer with the client
- Followed up with both clients and therapist to see if referrals were successful
- Did no follow-up

You can see the wide range of how therapists understand this issue. Even when they agree about the need to provide continuing care, they do it in assorted ways. Some therapists work hard to find, vet, and provide referrals for those clients who need to continue treatment; others offer clients only general suggestions for continued care, such as listing three or more clinics, group practices, or online directories; still others help clients articulate what they want in terms of continued treatment but leave the search and contact in the hands of the client.

If you believe that making referrals is part of your responsibility, be sure to leave time on your calendar. For example, some special needs clients are a challenge for continued care options due to the lack of providers with special expertise. One therapist in New York City complained that referrals for specialists to treat autistic children in her caseload are few and far between, and they usually have full practices and long waiting lists.

Sometimes it's difficult to find referrals that are providers for the insurance used by a client. A therapist who saw Medicare clients found that the dwindling number of therapists in her locale who worked as Medicare providers made finding referrals almost impossible. After trying hard to place a dozen clients during the last year of her practice and being unsuccessful, she finally had to tell her remaining clients that they were "on their own" in terms of finding continuing care, despite her strong concerns about their need for further treatment. This was her biggest regret about retiring, and although she worked to help her clients clarify the qualities that they wanted in a new therapist, she could not guarantee finding a provider that they could afford.

With this variety of referral approaches, you will need to decide what is best for your clients based on your philosophy of service, experience, training, and the norms of your licensure. If you are retiring suddenly, finding referrals for your entire caseload may not be possible. If you already have written policies or commitments in existence about how and when you make referrals, do your best to adhere to them.

Document your actions and decisions regarding referrals; note any and all conversations with therapists you have contacted, as well as client acceptance or denial of referrals you make. Keep these notes in the file you are compiling about your practice ending, in case questions about these decisions come up later.

ACTION STEP: Make a list of the referrals that you need to make before your retirement. How will you approach this with clients?

____

____

____

____

____

____

7. Conclude your business operation and notify permitting, administrative, accounting, business, and clinical affiliations, as well as any parties with whom you've made legal or financial agreements.

In this step are all the other aspects of your business operation. Begin to make a list of the permits and registrations your business works under, including the online platforms, services, consultants, and advisers that contribute to your management. Decide how and when to bring each item of the list to completion. Agreements you have made over the course of operating your practice need to be reviewed and concluded with steps such as these:

- Alert the local or state entity that issued your business license or permit of operation and begin the process of stoppage, including any DBAs (doing business as) where applicable
- Notify stakeholders (e.g., investors, partners, staff, suppliers) with time to exit agreements well
- Notify hospital or clinic affiliations
- Call, email, or write to your ongoing referral sources
- Retrieve data on any practice management systems in use, such as Simple Practice, and then end the ongoing service contract
- Export names and data; retain your lists of subscribers from digital platforms like Constant Contact or other teaching platforms like Coursera
- Withdraw your business information from payment platforms such as Square, Ivy, or Stripe
- End billing and payroll services
- Collect unpaid fees or outstanding payments from clients and insurance companies and address any and all outstanding legal or financial obligations associated with your business entity
- Decide when to stop using business credit cards

Other accounting and business, legal, or financial changes may require hiring professional advisers. At this point you will want to consult your accountant and will possibly need a lawyer to restructure taxes or to help you dissolve your business entity. In chapter 8, we look at the business options that may apply if you want to close, sell, or transfer your practice.

ACTION STEP: Make a list of the operations you need to conclude before closing your practice. If needed, consider any adviser you may need.

____

____

____

8. Discontinue your marketing efforts, advertising, website, voicemail, online directory listings, and professional social media accounts.

As you complete your to-do list, the final items will reverse the efforts you have made to be visible to clients. It can be emotional to decide to become less conspicuous—if not invisible—as you close your practice. You might put your name into a search engine to see all the websites and directories where you appear. Which of these need alerts or notifications to remove your listings?

Decide when to stop all marketing and advertising campaigns. Review your social media accounts (e.g., Facebook, LinkedIn, YouTube, Instagram) to decide what to keep active and what to alter to reflect your change of status.

Decide when to stop voicemail and email accounts, as well as when to shut down your website or other points of contact that were necessary to filling and maintaining your status as an active therapist.

ACTION STEP: Make a list of all the areas from which you will need to remove your brand.

9. Know how to store and ultimately destroy records, documentation, and files.

As you close down your practice, make sure that your closing or transfer of treatment records for your clients are clear and complete. The following information is helpful to include for each client:

- Summary of the case, including a diagnosis and a treatment plan
- Progress or lack of progress in meeting a treatment plan
- Transfer or closing plans and follow-up recommendation

Pay attention to the storage of your clinical records. Due to our litigious society, keeping clinical records long enough and disposing of them correctly is critical to preventing a malpractice lawsuit or other legal actions you and your practice might face after you have retired.

Legal experts advise that you cannot rely only on your state's statute of limitations or statute of repose to protect you from legal actions. Statutes relating to malpractice actions against therapists would not be applicable in litigation resulting from complaints or allegations involving fraud, conspiracy, criminal acts, or federal laws, rules, and regulations, as federal laws often have different requirements from state laws in terms of record protection.

Some medical boards are starting to insist that patient records be available whenever needed; this can mean from five to seven years, or in some cases, indefinitely. With this level of confusion and uncertainty, you should consult your professional association about their recommendations. If you have unanswered concerns, ask for legal advice.

For example, the National Association of Social Work (2012) recommends that you retain your records indefinitely in the event a malpractice suit arises against you later. Proper storage of paper records means that special safeguards should be taken to protect them in a dry, secure, fireproof file cabinet or other container at home, or in a storage space at a facility.

In your professional will, establish your written policies and procedures not only for storing patient and client records, but also for *destroying* those records safely when they are no longer required to be kept.

How might you destroy your clinical records when you deem it is the proper time? Disposal of paper medical records usually involves cross-cut shredding or burning. If you store records electronically, security measures for storage, set in the Health Insurance Portability and Accountability Act of 1996 (HIPAA), may include encryption software and firewalls. These records can be stored with an emergency backup file in the event of a natural disaster or other emergency.

When it comes time to destroy these records, be sure to purge them from your hard drive, and again, document what steps you have taken to protect confidential information, when you took them, and why.

ACTION STEP: Create a detailed plan for how you will store client records after your practice is closed.

10. Understand the value of having a professional will in the case you are unable to continue your clinical practice due to your death, illness, or other incapacity.

Unless you are retiring today, consider creating a professional will. Imagine if your practice needs to close suddenly due to your death or extreme illness: Who will contact your clients and how will they reach them? What should they do about your clinical records and their storage? Without a will, decisions will be made by others, possibly those less qualified than you, and these choices may be made under great stress.

A professional will is your best option to retain control of how your practice ends if it closes unexpectedly (Groshong, 2023). Just like having a personal will, having a professional will in place is a great kindness for others who succeed you. You can create your will and put it in safe keeping long before you will need it. A professional will appoint an executor to carry out your professional tasks and functions should you be unable to continue your clinical practice due to your death, illness, or other incapacity. The will compiles all your relevant data on the practice and informs the executor where to locate that data. It lists clients, insurance companies, colleagues, and associations who will need to know about your status. The will also defines how records are to be kept and protects sensitive client information.

Like any other legal document, there is legal language suggested for a professional will. After it's completed, its signing should be witnessed and can be notarized. Free forms for a professional will can be found online, including from these services:

- National Association of Social Workers: https://naswassurance.org/pdf/Example-of-a-Professional-Will.pdf
- American Psychological Association Services: https://www.apaservices.org/practice/business/management/sample-professional-will.pdf

A professional will is generally easy to create and essentially requires compiling information in one place that is easy for others to find. First, determine your will's executor.

Your Executor

It takes thought to determine who will be your executor. This is a position that requires a person's time and energy, so you need to consider who is appropriate for this task. Then talk with them ahead of time to see if they will accept this role. You *don't* need to assign this task to another licensed therapist. You can ask a trusted assistant or administrator to be responsible for executing most aspects of your will.

The will is going to provide detailed instructions for the executor, including the compiled information for making phone calls or sending letters of notification. Your executor will need to respect HIPAA regulations in terms of handling client files, but that can be accomplished by following the security rules of the U.S. Department of Health and Human Services, which requires covered entities (e.g., your executor) to maintain reasonable and appropriate administrative, technical, and physical safeguards for protecting client information. You know your practice best. If this role will require significant time and energy, establish compensation for the executor ahead of time.

What Is Involved in Being a Therapist's Executor?

Robyn Miller, founder of Theraclosure.com, a professional executor service for therapists, first found herself in the role of executor unexpectedly—she was tasked with carrying out the role by a close colleague who was suddenly diagnosed with a serious cancer. A practicing therapist for nearly twenty-five years, Miller (personal communication, 2024) explains that the executor role can vary in complexity depending on the therapist's aspirations, philosophy, and active caseload. Closing her friend's practice was a daunting yet instructive task, highlighting how much is required from those who take on this responsibility. Miller estimates that it can take an executor up to fifty hours to close a single therapist's practice, including tasks such as gathering information, notifying clients, finding referrals, handling the retention of digital records, and managing various other administrative duties.

In her role as a professional executor, Miller conducts an extensive interview process as early as possible to ensure she fully understands a therapist's requests, the location of all relevant information, passwords for accounts, and the preferred process for notifying clients.

If your executor is not a trained professional, but rather a friend or colleague, Miller cautions that one of the most difficult challenges is that both the executor and the therapist's clients will be grieving as the process unfolds. The emotional strain of informing clients about the death of a colleague while also grieving yourself can make this role particularly difficult to assume.

Once you identify who will be your executor, begin to compile the following:

- **Contact information:** Provide your executor with clear, detailed information on how to contact your clients, associates, interns, peers, support professionals, electronic mailing list, and other professional contacts who will need to be notified in the event of your death or inability to continue your clinical practice. Keep this in an organized, up-to-date file so that it is easy for your executor to find what they need. Provide your executor with the message you want them to use for notification, one that protects client confidentiality, explains the reason for the notification, and notes that you have approved the executor who is sending it.
- **Business information:** Compile the names and contact information of your attorney, accountant, landlord, insurance provider contracts, malpractice insurance policies, licensing board, and any other professional information that

is part of your practice. Have clear directions for what the executor should do or say to close your business accounts.

- **Recordkeeping:** Inform the executor where to locate all your client files, business data, tax statements, and other records that are part of your clinical practice. To do this, research your state and federal requirements about recordkeeping, but also consider recommendations from your professional associations based on your specific licensure. Revisit step 9, on how to dispose of client records, documents and files if that is part of the executor's job.

ACTION STEP: Make a list of information an executor of your will may need to know.

—*Exercise*—

Your Retirement Checklist

Check the following items that you have completed. Put a star by those which are next on your list to achieve:

- ❐ Make a retirement timeline, use a calendar, and have a corresponding budget for your plan.
- ❐ Clarify your licensure's ethical codes about ending your practice.
- ❐ Review contracts to alert insurance panels, landlords, licensing boards, and professional associations in a timely manner.
- ❐ Consider getting "tail" malpractice coverage.
- ❐ Compose a message and determine the timing for notifying existing, past, or potential clients.
- ❐ Find referrals for existing clients who need continued care.
- ❐ Conclude your business operation and notify permitting, administrative, accounting, business, and clinical affiliations, as well as any parties with whom you've made legal or financial agreements.
- ❐ Discontinue your marketing efforts, advertising, website, voicemail, online directory listings, and professional social media accounts.
- ❐ Know how to store and ultimately destroy records, documentation, and files.
- ❐ Understand the value of having a professional will in case you are unable to continue your clinical practice due to your death, illness, or other incapacity.

Moving Forward

We understand that this chapter's ten-step retirement guide will take time to work through and may prompt you to seek additional consultation. Use your retirement journal to explore your thoughts and feelings as you go through the steps to complete your plan. While it's normal to experience feelings of loss or anxiety as you recognize the gravity and comprehensiveness of this plan to close your practice, we hope you will also gain a sense of confidence in knowing you are taking the necessary steps. Each step you complete will help you feel more secure as you prepare to conclude your life's work.

In the next chapter, we explore saying goodbye to the business side of therapy. Some therapists take great pride in the business aspects of owning a practice, leading or managing an organization, or directing efforts to create, define, and produce programs and projects. We will guide you through the process of stepping back from these business-oriented roles with the care and attention they deserve.

—Chapter 8—

Your Business, Your Self

I (Lynn) remember one December morning when my husband came home early from his job as an architect in a small local firm.

"Did you get the day off?" I asked.

"In a way," he answered ruefully.

Due to a recession in the area's construction business, he had been laid off. Recently licensed as a clinical social worker, I had a very small private practice with only a handful of clients. I was enjoying a respite from the years of graduate school and getting licensing hours, and I liked barely working. But as my husband began his ultimately successful job search, I knew I had to get busy. It was time to grow my solo private practice. The good news was that prior to graduate school, I had spent years employed in the family business, so I knew exactly what to do.

That same week, I drafted a marketing plan. I followed the steps carefully, and soon, my caseload began to grow. Owning a practice required me to wear two hats: one as a therapist and the other as a business owner. I realized I needed to develop the nonclinical aspects of my practice with the same level of attention I gave to learning and applying my therapeutic skills. Fortunately, I had always been drawn to business, and I enjoyed the energy and creativity involved in entrepreneurship. Since I had previous business experience, working in small businesses and even trying to create a few of my own, I now applied what I knew to my private practice. Over time, I discovered that I could blend my passion for business with my dedication to therapy, which led me to another calling: teaching and writing about the business of therapy. Alongside my ongoing work as a clinician, I took on additional roles: business owner, teacher, author, consultant, and business coach.

You may have encountered a similar situation in your career, where you've taken on multiple roles in addition to the one for which you were initially trained.

Therapists often assume various responsibilities beyond counseling and treatment. They may own and operate small or large practices or work in agencies, clinics, nonprofits, foundations, public organizations, or academia. As they embrace these additional roles, their titles and responsibilities naturally expand:

- If you own and operate a solo private practice, you probably spend time engaged in billing, marketing, networking, and promoting your services—by definition, you are an entrepreneur.
- If you work in an agency, you may also be a supervisor or trainer of less-experienced therapists.
- If you work at a nonprofit or a public organization, you may have progressed into management, directing teams, hiring staff, and developing projects.
- If you supplement treatment with teaching, you may be adjunct or tenured faculty in academia, planning classes and organizing curriculum.
- If you create new material, write books or articles, or teach others about methods of therapy, you may be an author, presenter, podcast host, or influencer.

If any of the previous descriptions resonate with your professional experience, it's important to recognize that having multiple roles can make the retirement process more complex. Your professional influence likely extends beyond individual clients, impacting colleagues, organizations, and possibly even broader community networks. In addition to considering the financial and logistical aspects of transitioning out of your primary clinical responsibilities, you must also address the potential effects your retirement could have on the systems and individuals who depend on your expertise, leadership, and presence.

As you navigate this transition, the interconnectedness of your various roles—whether in leadership, administrative, or community-based capacities—demands a more nuanced approach to retirement planning. It's essential to consider the continuity of operations, the delegation of responsibilities, and the potential long-term effects on the organizations and individuals you've mentored or influenced. The complexity of this process underscores the importance of a strategic, forward-thinking approach to retirement that accounts for both professional and personal considerations.

Closing a Bigger Door

Allie, a psychologist who started a small private practice after many years working for a nonprofit doing testing and assessments, explained, "At first I only knew how to hang out a shingle and print up a business card and hope that some friends or colleagues would send me clients who needed testing. But eventually, I got busy. My practice filled and I wanted to expand to doing treatment too. As my little solo practice grew, I needed to hire associates. It evolved naturally, but having staff meant that I often lay awake at night thinking about payroll, intake systems, and advertising. I worried about my team's morale and finding ways to be a fair but profitable employer. Eventually I realized that I just loved having a business, and guess what? I think I am good at it!"

Today Allie's practice has twenty associates with four administrative staff in three leased locations around her city. "I am now ready to retire. I am almost eighty and I need to stop working, but I don't want to just walk away from what I have built. The business has held so much of my hopes and dreams and contains a lot of what I believe about clinical methods, equity, and ethics. Now I wonder at night, what can I do to make sure that this business survives beyond my retirement?"

Whether or not you have a large business, you likely still hold multiple roles within your practice. Even in a solo practice, the various tasks and responsibilities you've taken on are still significant parts of your overall career. Each role you've assumed contributes to the broader scope of your professional journey, reflecting your growth and the skills you've developed along the way.

Roger, a licensed professional counselor, has a small solo practice and no desire to expand. "I am thinking about retirement in a few years, but it seems sad to me that my practice will fold. It's too small to sell and it's basically just me, so I can't imagine I can transfer it to another therapist. But I built a business. I have made enough money to support myself and my family. I stretched myself beyond what I was originally trained to do and it paid off for me. I know I will have very sad feelings when it is time to close the door for the last time."

It can help to review your career progression in order to claim the full scope of your capacities and multiple roles.

—*Exercise*—

Your Career Progression

Use this exercise to chart your career progression in linear form, starting with your first job after your graduate degree all the way to the present. Include all the important markers, changes, and achievements that got you from where you were to where you are today. The following list of questions will help you build a timeline of your entire career. Use the additional space to write about the following questions as you recall the important aspects of your education, training, and work situations.

After completing your graduate degree, how did you earn the hours you needed for licensure?

____

____

____

What was the early work experience like for you? What went well, what did you learn, what did you take away from the first steps of your career?

____

____

____

What did you do after licensure? Did this stage of postlicensure begin to define your career or offer you new skills as an entrepreneur, manager, teacher, or supervisor?

____

____

____

How do you define the nonclinical aspects of your work? What skills are essential to your income and effectiveness in that area separate from therapeutic methods?

What did you need to develop internally to allow yourself to succeed in an expanded career? What strengths did you acquire? What challenges were you faced with?

When you retire, what will you need to let go of in terms of skills, talents, and abilities that are essential to your nonclinical role?

When you retire, who (e.g., associates, mentors, bosses, employees) will you say goodbye to? How do you feel about this part of letting go?

What will be the most challenging part of ending your nonclinical roles or positions when you retire?

Your Career Progression
Retirement
Graduate Degree

When you are done creating your timeline, note the thoughts, feelings, and responses you have to seeing your work from this perspective.

Do you feel satisfied with the work you have done, or is there more you need to do or delegate to others in order to feel fulfilled?

___

___

___

What needs to be added or closed down to help you to feel that your career is complete?

___

___

___

Matty, a clinical social worker, reviewed her career path after mapping it out. "Look way back here," she told us, pointing toward the left edge of the sheet. "I started out as a clinical social worker, interning in a large community mental health clinic. Then I got licensed, but I stayed at the clinic. I had a big caseload, but my door was open between sessions to support other therapists who were having a hard day."

Her finger traced the timeline. "Then I was hired by a nonprofit hospital with a psychiatric wing. I was promoted to become a clinical supervisor and then clinical director of social work services. I learned about managing up and how to get comfortable with my own ideas and authority. I took courses to develop my leadership skills. You can see how my duties and functions expanded here."

At the edge of the paper, she showed us another position, at the foundation she now works for. "It looks like the branches of a tree. Each new position spreads out a bit, because I keep learning more. I have been with this foundation for ten years; given my age, the board is urging me to find and train my successor."

Later, after reviewing her graphic representation, Matty talked about the process of letting go, using a metaphor to explain how she feels about being replaced in her position when she retires. "To think about letting go of all of this, I am going to imagine that I am in a relay race. I've run my part well, but now I need to pass the baton to the next person. I am always part of a team, and now I must hold out my hand to aid the next runner."

After you review your career progression, it can help you to find a metaphor, like Matty did, to encourage your acceptance of releasing what has been so meaningful to you personally, professionally, and financially. She chose a sport metaphor. Others we have coached use experiences that reflect what is familiar to their experience, like hobbies or passions. You might consider the never-ending flow of water in a river, the way a tree drops its leaves in the fall, or the end of a garden growing season, signaling that it is time to dig up the plants that are no longer bearing fruit and start over with refreshed soil.

RETIREMENT JOURNAL

Find a Metaphor for Letting Go

Create your own metaphor to symbolize letting go by using the following prompts:

- What metaphor could you use to help soothe the loss of leaving your work behind you?
- How does this metaphor help you to see your situation in a positive context?
- Does the metaphor evoke some new insight about retirement?

Selling or Transferring a Private Practice

When you've built a small business like a private practice, there are additional financial options to consider when you retire. If you're retiring from an active practice that you own and operate, you may wonder if there is any alternative to shutting it down. Can a private practice be sold or transferred?

I (Lynn) have taught many workshops about the business of therapy, and whenever I get to the topic of building a practice to sell, therapists usually ask, *Who would want to buy an existing practice instead of starting one from scratch?* For some, purchasing an established practice is a shortcut to launching their own, and in many cases, it can be more profitable than investing the time, cost, and energy required to build one from the ground up. A buyer might be new to the area or profession and want to benefit from the groundwork you've already laid. They may also find it difficult to break into a specialized market, and if you've built a strong reputation, the buyer can capitalize on your visibility.

Surprisingly, even a small solo practice can have valuable assets that attract potential buyers. What assets could your practice possess? You may have developed a proven method that gets results and is in demand, created workshops or programs that sell, built a reputation for specialized services that could be handed off to another trained therapist, or established successful marketing strategies that consistently bring in clients—these are all highly valuable assets that might be transferred or sold to another owner.

If you are preparing for retirement and want to sell or transfer your practice, it usually takes several years to position the practice and begin to develop a pipeline of potential buyers. If this is something you are considering, even if you are not sure about the decision, there are still actions you can begin completing now.

—*Exercise*—

Selling a Private Practice

If you have sold a home, you have some idea of what it is like to sell a practice. Even if you love your home and it contains many important memories, to a new buyer, it's just a property. Your practice may represent your best work and creativity; it may have generated decades of goodwill; you may have changed hundreds or thousands of lives. But at sale, it will be assessed as a business. Get support and consider hiring an intermediary to help with the process if it is hard for you to be objective.

If you plan to consider selling your practice, prepare the following:

1. **Documentation**
   a. Record your annual income and expense history for the previous five years.

   ____

   ____

   ____

   ____

   b. Include measures of new client calls or contacts.

   ____

   ____

   ____

   ____

   c. Note average client stay.

   ____

   ____

   ____

   ____

d. Note average client yield in terms of income.

____

____

____

____

e. Document any measures you have of client satisfaction.

____

____

____

____

f. Compile results of pre-and post-surveys.

____

____

____

____

2. **Transferable assets**
   a. Don't assume that you, the therapist and the primary asset of the practice, are not replaceable.
   b. Calculate exactly what you do and how you do it so a buyer can replicate your success.
   c. Note how you attract clients, a process that you could teach a buyer to do equally well.
   d. Write a manual to help a buyer reproduce your results, both clinically and operationally.
   e. Become a good reporter and researcher; understand your outcomes, and then find a way to help a buyer succeed too.
   f. Note transferable assets, including practice name, website, marketing materials, clinical training materials and programs,

management practices, administration policies, procedures, mailing list, and possibly real estate (if you own your office).

3. **Valuation**

   a. To determine what your practice is worth, remember the difference between value and price: Value is usually subjective—in the eye of the seller; buyers focus on price.

   b. Therapy practices usually sell for less than a medical practice might, but if you have a strong income history, you may be able to ask for several times that annual income.

   c. Value the practice using a formula that includes the annual income. For example: (annual income × 2) + additional valued items and transferable assets

4. **Position for sale**

   a. Bring all of these elements together to make a case for the sale of the practice.

   b. Look at practice listings online that medical brokers use.

   c. Write a summary describing your practice, its value, and its transferable assets in a way that is appealing and accurate.

   d. Hire a medical broker or agent to help you advertise your practice for sale.

One therapist we interviewed spent years developing a group practice with a high profile in her community and is now planning her retirement. She is in the process of closing the practice in a way that's uncommon but commendable. Rather than put it up for sale to an outside bidder, she is transferring her business, at a significantly discounted price, to the remaining therapists in the group. It will then be employee owned. She discussed not just the valuation of her practice, but also the way she wants to honor the contributions of the therapists whose work was so important to the overall practice success. She has brought in a specialized financial adviser with legal expertise in business sales, to examine options. She hopes to deed the business and office property to her associates and to price it with long payout plans so it is affordable to the therapists in the group. She wants them to have a stake in the success of the practice by becoming owners together. Her biggest hope is that the programs and guiding principles that defined the practice will continue, even without her presence.

Letting Go as a Leader

You may not own a private practice, but instead hold another type of influential leadership role. Besides being the owner of a solo or group practice, leadership for therapists can include holding any of the following roles:

- Founder of an adjunct, nonclinical business
- Supervisor, executive, or director in a nonprofit, clinic, foundation, or agency
- Titled role in a public or private organization
- Board member, adviser, or leadership of a volunteer association
- Content creator, author, writer, presenter, host, speaker, or trainer
- Faculty at a school, university, or college
- Consultant, adviser, or forensic expert working with other high-level professionals

—Exercise—

Business Skills Checklist

As you face retirement, preserve the positive experience of the investment of energy, skills, and training that you have made in all areas of your career.

1. The following list includes skills you may have accrued in your nontherapeutic roles and duties.
2. Check the ones that you have used and relied upon to further your work. Add others that may not be listed.
3. Put a star by any of the skills you would miss in retirement and want to transfer to other aspects of your life.
4. When you're finished, start a new list of all the skills you've marked with a star. Next to each, list possible options for places, people, and additional activities that would be a good fit in retirement. This might be volunteer-based or informal groups, associations tied to your hobbies or passions, or perhaps something new that you will now have time to develop.

Skills

- ❐ Strategic planning
- ❐ Innovating
- ❐ Delegating
- ❐ Administrating
- ❐ Creating programs or policies
- ❐ Preparing budgets
- ❐ Directing research
- ❐ Resolving conflicts
- ❐ Organizing conferences or events
- ❐ Facilitating meetings
- ❐ Setting goals
- ❐ Defining a multiyear vision, purpose, and mission statement
- ❐ Hiring and firing
- ❐ Conducting performance reviews

- ❒ Negotiating with vendors, departments, or boards
- ❒ Overseeing allocation
- ❒ Documenting and reporting
- ❒ Marketing
- ❒ Networking
- ❒ Creating training
- ❒ Presenting material
- ❒ Writing and publishing
- ❒ Increasing profit or income, investing, or managing finances
- ❒ Buying, selling, bartering, or trading
- ❒ Connecting people with resources
- ❒ Lobbying governmental organizations
- ❒ Organizing
- ❒ Managing data and measures
- ❒ Presenting, speaking, or training
- ❒ Other: ______________________

  ____

Skills for Use in Retirement

- ______________________________
- ______________________________
- ______________________________
- ______________________________
- ______________________________
- ______________________________
- ______________________________
- ______________________________
- ______________________________
- ______________________________

Leaders' Feelings about Leaving

Leaders' feelings about leaving may involve a mix of apprehension and uncertainty. After Andrea got licensed as a psychologist, she specialized in forensic consultation. She eventually joined a legal firm, and to her delight, she became a partner. She was proud of the teams she had fostered and the programs she'd created. At the age of sixty-nine, she began to think seriously about retirement. The time and energy demanded by her job were difficult to manage. But like many leaders, she felt emotional about leaving. Andrea had doubts about whether her programs would survive without her. "What if this all falls apart when I leave?" she worried.

Andrea called a colleague who had retired from another organization a year earlier and had some wisdom to pass on. She told Andrea that organizations are usually built around programs, not people. "We are both therapists at our core," her mentor reminded her. "Part of successful retirement is finding a way to work through all of your feelings."

Here are some of the most common emotions we hear from those therapists in leadership roles as they prepare for retirement. See if any one of these, or a combination of them, affirms your own experience:

- **Loss:** If you have given a lot of yourself to your work, you may feel a loss of purpose when it's time to retire. If your career is central to how you see your value in the world, retiring can feel like a forfeiture of an important part of yourself. (See chapter 3 for a review of ways to rebalance your sense of self.)
- **Relief:** Leadership comes with pressure; you may experience a lasting sense of relief when you retire. Managing your responsibilities, problem-solving, and meeting the demands of people can be a burden you are happy to remove from your shoulders.
- **Nostalgia:** Retirement can bring sadness or a sense of nostalgia. You may find yourself reminiscing about all you have done and the relationships you formed. Seeing the organization evolve without your continuing input can be emotionally difficult. The chapters in section IV of this book can help you find ways to shift your energy toward a good future.
- **Uncertainty:** For some therapists, stepping into a new phase of life without the structure and routine of work can feel disorienting. You may worry about how you

will fill your time, or fear losing the sense of achievement and validation that came from your professional accomplishments. (We will address this in chapter 11.)

- **Doubt:** You may feel a sense of guilt when retiring, especially if you have built something significant that you feel you are leaving behind. You might worry about letting down employees, partners, or others who rely on you. There might also be self-doubt about whether you've made the right decision or whether you are leaving too soon. (See chapter 10 to help you claim all you have contributed.)
- **Fulfillment:** For many therapists, retirement can bring a deep sense of accomplishment, especially when you recognize how many people you have helped and assisted during your long career. Retiring can actually help you feel more gratitude because you have time to savor and look back with pride on your achievements, the impact you made, and the relationships you built.
- **Excitement:** Maybe your days are filled with ideas and plans as you count down the remaining time. For some, retirement means the luxury of open time to be with family, travel, or even relocate. Are you eager to stop working and immerse yourself in a beloved project, hobby, new skill, or area of talent? If so, you may be feeling excited and joyful as you plan to retire.

Leadership usually combines a high level of responsibility with a good number of benefits. These benefits can include the ability to impact and influence the direction of a clinic, nonprofit, association, or public or private organization. If you are a leader and find it hard to leave the benefits conferred on your position, you may enjoy the recognition and prestige. Or you may appreciate the autonomy of being able to make key decisions or the financial rewards associated with this.

If you are currently in a leadership role, what aspects do you most appreciate and enjoy? What will make it difficult for you to step down?

RETIREMENT JOURNAL

Leadership Reflections

If you are having trouble letting go of your role, status, and responsibilities, along with the pleasure and productivity of your work, reflect on the following prompts in your retirement journal:

- What part of leadership did you like best?
- What are you grateful for from your leadership experience?
- What part of leadership are you glad to drop?
- Where will you place your leadership energy in retirement?
- How can you lean into the inevitable loss?
- What does the present day hold in terms of opportunity for rest and renewal?
- What is a creative endeavor that can give the transition meaning for you?

Moving Forward

Now it's time for one more essential piece of preparation: Do you have a retirement budget? Do you know how much you'll need in your savings accounts or investments to retire comfortably? It's time to talk about money.

If you're feeling uncomfortable and tempted to skip the next chapter, you're not alone. Money can be a complicated and emotionally charged issue for anyone—not just therapists. For therapists, especially those in private practice who may struggle to balance profit and service, money can feel like an unwelcome topic. But your ability to navigate financial matters effectively is crucial for preparing for a safe and comfortable retirement.

In the next chapter, we want to have an open conversation with you about your finances and provide you with information and resources that will help you plan for a good retirement.

—Chapter 9—

Money Maturity

Money can be a complicated and emotionally charged issue for anyone, not just therapists. I (Lynn) remember watching an early Madonna documentary, *Truth or Dare*, in 1991. In the film, Madonna lets the camera follow her everywhere: backstage as she prepares for a performance, into her bedroom where her tour dancers are lounging in various stages of undress, and even to the doctor's office to check on her sore throat. But at one point, she puts up a hand and says to the cameraman, "Stop." Where does she go that the camera can no longer follow? To her accountant!

It's a moment that underscores how even those at the top of their game have boundaries around money and finances, a topic that often feels private and charged. For therapists, especially those in private practice who struggle to reconcile profit (the business side) and service (the heart of our work), money can feel like an unwelcome topic.

For example, in my role as a business coach, when I initiate conversations with therapists about their practice finances, I often encounter a lack of awareness. When I ask questions—"How much does your practice earn each month? Do you feel financially secure? Is this where you thought you'd be, money-wise, at this point in your career?"—the response is often silence or unease. It's clear that many therapists haven't fully engaged with their financial reality, and that discomfort can make it even harder to approach retirement planning with confidence.

As you approach retirement, a lack of financial knowledge or maturity can leave you vulnerable. But what do I mean by *money maturity*? Think about how you feel when managing your finances, whether it's balancing your checkbook, reviewing your profit and loss statement, or handling investments. Many people feel inexperienced—almost like a teenager—when it comes to managing their money.

However, true financial maturity isn't about age; it's about your level of financial education. It's about how comfortable and confident you feel navigating various financial situations. Your ability to manage your finances effectively is crucial for preparing for a safe and comfortable retirement. The more informed you are, the more empowered you will be to make decisions that align with your long-term goals.

For example, if you avoid thinking or talking about money, are unaware of your income and expenses, haven't prioritized saving, or haven't created a retirement budget or gathered essential information, you're not approaching your financial stability with the maturity it deserves for retirement. In this chapter, we want to have an open conversation with you about your finances and give you information and resources that will help you plan for retirement.

To begin, it's helpful to understand any early beliefs that shape your current views on money—beliefs that may be holding you back from becoming fully resourceful. The psychology of money explores your thoughts and feelings about finance, including those unconscious beliefs that may influence your daily actions. As you work through this process, you'll learn to shift from emotional responses to more logical, deliberate, and informed financial decisions.

We hope this chapter helps you move forward with confidence, enabling you to be prepared and at peace with your financial retirement goals and objectives.

Understanding Your Relationship with Money

The issue of money and retirement can be emotionally complex. While working with an adviser provides you with facts, applying those facts to make decisions can be more challenging than you might expect—unless you're aware of your own relationship with money. Understanding how your emotions and beliefs influence your financial choices is key to making informed decisions.

I (Margaret) have always believed in abundance—that there is enough in the world for me to survive and even thrive—and I have made it a spiritual tenet to live by. No matter how little money was available, I felt confident I would be all right—I simply trusted I could make my circumstances work. So when I found myself dragging my feet about choosing when to retire, I did not at first realize it had anything to do with money. I had saved money; my financial adviser indicated that I could retire without worrying about paying my bills. So why was it feeling so hard for me to take the next step?

A conversation with Lynn brought this dilemma into sharp focus. Putting on her business coaching hat, she explained to me how the money mindset shaped in a person's childhood—including how one does or does not see examples of how to earn, spend, save, and invest with intention and purpose—can influence the way they set up their therapy practice or manage their business plan. Suddenly, it felt like a key turned in my mind, unlocking the resistance I didn't even know I had. I didn't want to give up the control I had that allowed me to earn more money if or when I needed it. I wanted the ongoing power to take on more clients or teach another seminar "just in case."

What I realized from Lynn's teaching was that my childhood model of money was operating unconsciously, in the background, yet still influencing my financial choices. It was a powerful revelation—understanding that my mindset around money wasn't just about the present, but rooted in past experiences that were shaping my approach to financial decisions.

I was the middle child of nine siblings. We always had a nice home and enough to eat; since this was in the 1950s and '60s, there was no expectation that big families would eat out at restaurants or go on vacations, so I did not feel as if I was missing out on anything, even things that my peers experienced. But there were limits. Every month, Mom worked out how much—and which bills—to pay. With all those children, Dad's income as a salesman did not always stretch to stay current on a mortgage, gas, clothing, and medical bills. Even as a child, I could sense tension around having enough money to stay afloat.

Dad was good at earning but not good at budgeting. If he wanted something, his explicitly stated attitude was *I will just work a little more.* And he did. He made an extra sale. I watched and learned. My sense of abundance was not just based on a spiritual commitment, I realized—it had also taken root and blossomed by observing how Dad just worked harder and came up with the income he wanted, month after month. I had so completely absorbed this as a financial model that I never realized it: As an adult, my approach to my business and my financial capacity mirrored his.

Whenever I worried about paying for my kid's college or needed a bit more money to spend on gifts, I simply took on more work. I worked harder to come up with the income I wanted and needed. Unlike Mom, I earned enough to pay off bills every month and save for retirement without having to scrimp. But without realizing how my childhood experience affected me, I simply believed that, like Dad, I would always earn enough—and that I *could* always earn more. As long as I kept working.

When I thought about retiring, an inner voice recoiled. How could I trust I would have enough money if I could not earn? Until that talk with Lynn, I did not understand my inability to consider a life without the potential to just "work a little more." Once I understood the impact of the parental modeling, I was able to make rational evaluations of my needs and my available resources that allowed me to finally step away from my work.

Your Money Beliefs

If you find the topic of money troublesome, you're not alone. Thinking about money, formulating a plan, and then taking responsible action can be difficult. In fact, a poll by the National Endowment for Financial Education (2021) found that 40 percent of respondents admit to having "money infidelity"—lying to their partner about what they save or spend. Issues and trauma related to money often begin in childhood and can persist throughout a lifetime.

These deep-seated feelings around money can make it hard to engage with financial planning, even when it's essential to your future security. Understanding and addressing the emotional and psychological factors at play is an important step in developing a healthier relationship with money.

Money beliefs formed in childhood can influence your adult personal and professional life in both obvious and subtle ways (Grodzki, 2015). Frustratingly, these beliefs may remain active and continue to affect you regardless of your current financial situation or wealth. Negative beliefs, in particular, can undermine your ability to plan effectively for retirement. Understanding and addressing any psychological factors that may interfere with your ability to achieve a safe and secure retirement is crucial.

For example, perhaps you grew up in a family in which money was prized above all else, and you saw how much importance was placed on wealth. As a result, you might find yourself constantly thinking about money and focusing on earning as much as possible. This mindset can carry over into your professional life; maybe you're willing to see clients you don't particularly enjoy, as long as they pay your full fee. You might take on an exhausting caseload of fifty hours a week, driven by the pressure to keep earning more, even though you may not truly need to.

This relentless drive to earn can lead to burnout, making you dream of having less stress, quitting your job, or finding something less demanding. But, because you're so focused on maintaining an income, you may not know how to allow retirement to unfold. The fear of letting go of the financial security you've worked so hard for can make it difficult to embrace the transition, even when it's time to move on.

Alternatively, consider a different scenario. Maybe money scares you. If you witnessed your parents' anxiety about finances, you may feel anxious whenever money becomes the topic. In your role as a therapist, you might feel conflict-averse when discussing money—finding it difficult to negotiate a better rent or enforce your cancellation policy. Clients may push you to slide your fee, and landlords might easily convince you to pay too much. For you, anything related to money becomes painful and difficult to navigate. In retirement, you worry that you will not be able to set boundaries financially or stick with a pre-arranged financial plan.

To prepare yourself to handle money with more wisdom and logic, it helps to first understand the beliefs that may be operating in the background. Let's dive a little deeper into the three most common challenging money beliefs: deprivation, dissociation, and demonization.

Deprivation

Perhaps you grew up experiencing true financial deprivation, where there was never enough money to meet your basic needs. Your parents may have argued or worried about money every week, and this anxiety affected everyone in the house. Even though you may not be experiencing deprivation now, the belief that money is scarce could still be active within you. You might carry the idea that money should be watched closely, and you may be reluctant to spend on anything deemed "unnecessary."

In your professional life as a therapist, this belief can influence your decisions. For example, you avoid attending important conferences because they feel too expensive. You frustrate colleagues sharing office space with you by refusing to cover even small amenities like magazines, flowers, or bottled water to make the waiting room more inviting. You skip joining professional associations because they don't seem cost-effective. As a result, you are depriving your business of the resources it needs to grow, let alone thrive. You miss networking opportunities, focus too much on finding the cheapest deals, cut corners on advertising, skip valuable training, or struggle to understand that sometimes, you need to spend money to make money.

You might have the following thoughts:

- *I can't make money.*
- *I am just one step away from being on the street.*
- *I can't charge what I am worth because no one will pay my full fee.*
- *Money doesn't grow on trees.*

Dissociation

Perhaps you grew up feeling that money was a mystery. In your family, it seemed to appear out of nowhere, only to disappear just as quickly. When money was available, your family spent freely, but when debt piled up, panic set in. As a result, you may now find yourself on an emotional money rollercoaster.

This sense of mystery surrounding money may still be influencing your professional life. When you make money, you feel on top of the world, but when business slows down, you become self-critical and down. Your financial state directly affects your mood—you feel either blessed or panicked, but you're unsure of how to regain control. You may have never tracked your finances or reviewed a profit and loss statement for your practice. Your cash flow swings unpredictably between positive and negative, leaving you drained and unsure of how to stabilize your finances.

If the idea of money as a mystery is still present, you may find yourself unprepared to create a budget or take a close look at the money you'll need to plan for a secure retirement.

You might have the following thoughts:

- *Nice people don't talk about money.*
- *I only care about my craft—money isn't important.*
- *If I don't pay attention to money, it comes when I really need it.*
- *Money isn't everything—in fact, it isn't anything.*

Demonization

Perhaps you grew up in a family where money was never openly discussed—it was considered taboo or dirty. When you asked about prices, your parents told you to be quiet. When you wondered how much your father earned, you were sent out of the room for being rude. Money often led to arguments and was the cause of tears, upset, or worse. You might have even wished money could just disappear. As a result, you hate looking at your bank statements and avoid any situation involving money that might require conflict or confrontation. At the heart of this may be a childhood belief that money is inherently evil.

In your professional life, you may say, "I don't like to think about money. I just love being a therapist. I wish money didn't matter." As a result, you feel uneasy whenever money comes up with a client. You struggle to raise your fees, don't bill on time, and carry the burden of unpaid accounts. You avoid checking your business account, feel embarrassed by how little you earn, and can't understand why you never seem to get ahead financially. With this belief, billing for your services becomes more than just a transaction—it feels like a judgment of your morals.

You might have the following thoughts:

- *Money is the root of all evil.*
- *I can't have money and have integrity too.*
- *Only greedy people think about money all the time.*
- *Money is dirty and corrupting.*

RETIREMENT JOURNAL

Your Thinking About Money

Consider your own money beliefs. Reflect on the following prompts in your retirement journal to explore how your childhood influenced your current thoughts surrounding money:

- Which of the three money beliefs mentioned previously feel most true to your childhood experience?
- Are they still active within you today?
- What professional situations may have exacerbated these beliefs? For example: Did you have an experience in a clinic, agency, or group practice that set up additional beliefs? Have your peers, support groups, supervisors, therapists, or mentors had beliefs that you have adopted? Are these beliefs affecting you positively or negatively?
- Do you also have positive and helpful ways of thinking about money?
- How do you feel about your financial future in retirement?

Resolving Negative Money Beliefs

The good news is that your money history is learned behavior. You can unlearn any unhelpful financial beliefs and replace old money messages that no longer serve you as an adult preparing to retire. The ability to advance and progress as we change beliefs and unlearn aspects of our history is part and parcel of the work we do as therapists.

George Kinder (1999), a financial life planner, sees money as a facilitator of one's personal evolution. He urges money to be a tool that allows people to transform themselves as they age and progress. In Kinder's book, *The Seven Stages of Money Maturity*, he identified seven stages of maturity in relation to money, starting with childhood and going into old age:

1. **Innocence:** The childhood stage, where money plays no significant role in our lives
2. **Pain:** The realization that some people have more money than we do, others have less, and life requires us to work for a living
3. **Knowledge:** The understanding of the importance of saving, budgeting, and investing money
4. **Understanding:** Coming to terms with our emotions surrounding greed, envy, and resentment
5. **Vigor:** The physical, emotional, and spiritual energy needed to achieve our financial goals
6. **Vision:** Tapping into our inner wisdom and seeking to contribute to the well-being of communities
7. **Aloha:** Practicing compassion and serving others without expecting anything in return.

—*Exercise*—

Find Your Level of Money Maturity

Using Kinder's seven stages of money maturity, answer the following questions.

Which stage applies to you at this time?

___

Which stage do you want to inhabit when you are retired?

___

If there is a gap between these two stages, what steps or actions do you need to take to reach the new level?

___

___

___

What resources (e.g., people, concepts, tools, ideas, etc.) can you bring to help you reach a new stage of money maturity?

___

___

___

What is your plan to move forward?

___

___

___

The goal of money maturity is to remove negative emotions (e.g., fear, anger, pity, resentment, anxiety, guilt, shame) from your financial decisions and replace them with clear thinking and a sense of resourcefulness. Being mature about money means that you can clarify your own philosophy and your personal and professional ethics, and add in data, analysis, common sense, and best business practices in all your financial dealings.

To achieve money maturity, it can help to think of financial development as similar to Maslow's (1943) hierarchy of needs, a motivational theory in psychology often represented as a pyramid that presents a five-tier model of human needs. The five levels are 1) survival (such as food and water), 2) safety, 3) love and belonging, 4) esteem, and 5) self-actualization. The theory suggests that lower-level needs, like basic survival, must be met before higher needs can be pursued.

While few individuals fully reach self-actualization, many experience peak moments of it. The order of the hierarchy isn't rigid—some people may prioritize esteem over love, or self-actualize despite lacking material wealth. In reality, our behaviors are often driven by multiple needs at once.

Maslow's Hierarchy of Needs

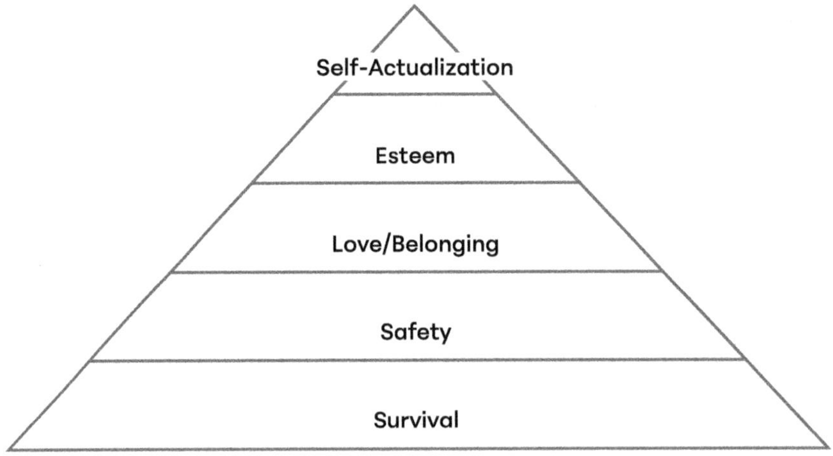

Now contrast Maslow's hierarchy to a similar pyramid of financial needs (Neufeld, 2020). You can see that like Maslow, the lower level of the financial pyramid is also concerned with survival. At this level, you are only focused on having enough money to meet your basic needs and keep food on the table or a roof over your head. The next level is one of safety: You can pay your bills, have some money saved for emergencies, and relax some. You sustain a lifestyle that is healthier and has less stress and worry.

The next level matches the Maslow idea of belonging to a larger community: Now you have enough money to save, invest, and donate to causes you believe in. You begin to build a nest egg, with money to pass down to the next generation of your family. The upper levels of financial independence and legacy or philanthropy are ways to begin to use money to further a sense of self-actualization. Money becomes a tool for self-fulfillment, exploration, benevolence, and humanitarianism. At these upper levels, money often takes on a new meaning. You feel safe and secure and now wonder how to make your money have a lasting effect in the greater world. You are in a position to make an impact via a gift of money to others.

Hierarchy of Financial Needs

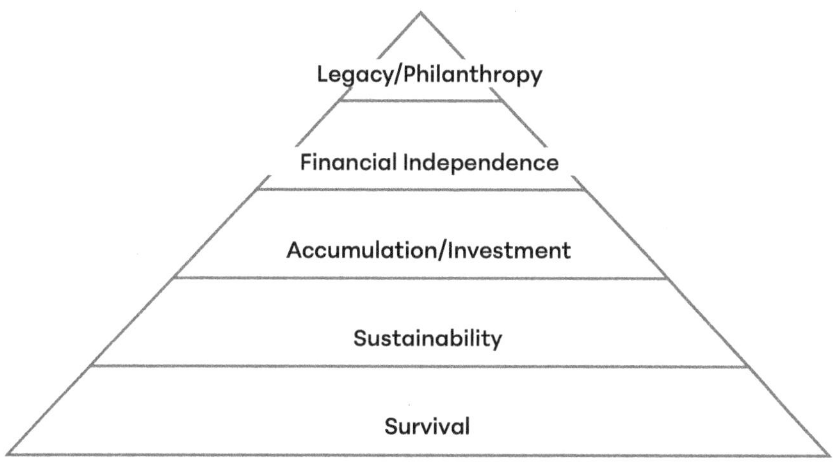

RETIREMENT JOURNAL

Pyramid of Needs: Where Do You Stand?

Consider your current place and where you may want to advance during retirement by reflecting on the following prompts in your retirement journal:

- What is your current level on the pyramid in terms of human needs? How do you feel about this level?
- What is your current level on the pyramid in terms of financial needs? How do you feel about this level?
- What is the level on each pyramid you would like to achieve?
- What would need to be different to achieve these levels? What steps can you take right now?

Making a Retirement Budget

The two of us are fans of living and working using a written financial budget. Budgeting for retirement is crucial because it gives you a clear picture of your financial future, helps you avoid surprises, ensures you can cover your living expenses, and allows you to make the most of your savings. It's a way to protect yourself from the risks of outliving your savings, overspending, or not having enough to enjoy your desired lifestyle. Creating a good budget in retirement depends on a variety of factors, like your lifestyle, your health care needs, and any existing sources of income. Without a solid budget, you're essentially navigating retirement without a roadmap, which can lead to unnecessary stress or even financial instability.

So, as fans of having a budget, here are our top twelve reasons why you would benefit too. A careful written retirement budget does all of the following:

1. **Ensures financial security:** By budgeting, you have a clearer understanding of how much money you'll need to cover your expenses in retirement, ensuring that you don't run into financial problems later on. It helps you align your spending with your income, giving you peace of mind that you can cover both essential and discretionary costs.
2. **Helps you plan for long-term needs:** Retirement can last twenty or thirty years, and budgeting allows you to plan for the long haul. You need to consider inflation, unexpected medical expenses, potential long-term care, and other long-term needs that might arise. Having a budget ensures you've saved enough for those situations.
3. **Prevents overspending:** Without a clear budget, it's easy to overspend or fail to account for certain costs (e.g., health care or taxes). A retirement budget helps you control how much you spend each month, allowing you to live within your means, avoid debt, and make sure your savings last.
4. **Maximizes your retirement savings:** Budgeting allows you to allocate your finances efficiently, whether you're saving for retirement or spending money. It helps you track your investments, decide how much to withdraw each year, and keep your financial goals in check. It also encourages you to keep an eye on investment returns, keeping your overall retirement strategy on track.
5. **Adapts to changing circumstances:** During retirement, your needs and goals may shift. A budget allows you to adjust to changes like health issues, lifestyle

shifts (e.g., downsizing or moving), or fluctuations in market conditions. It helps you remain flexible and adapt without compromising your financial security.

6. **Helps you maintain your desired lifestyle:** A good budget allows you to plan for the kind of retirement you want. Whether that includes travel, hobbies, or spending more time with family, a budget helps you ensure you have enough money to enjoy your retirement without financial stress.
7. **Prepares for health care costs:** Health care becomes a larger expense in retirement. Medicare doesn't cover everything, and additional health insurance or long-term care may be needed. A retirement budget helps you plan for these increased costs and avoid being caught off guard by medical bills.
8. **Provides a roadmap for decision-making:** When you have a detailed budget, it becomes easier to make informed decisions, whether you're choosing how to spend or save, how much to withdraw from your retirement accounts, or whether to make large purchases or take on additional expenses. You'll know exactly how much room you have in your budget.
9. **Mitigates financial risks:** Budgeting helps you avoid running out of money by balancing withdrawals with sustainable income. It allows you to manage the risk of outliving your savings and helps you adjust your financial strategy if your income or market returns fall short of expectations.
10. **Increases your confidence in retirement:** Knowing that you've planned ahead for your financial future can bring great peace of mind. A budget lets you see exactly where your money is going, how much is coming in, and where you can cut back if necessary, all of which helps reduce anxiety about money during retirement.
11. **Aids in tax planning:** Understanding your budget also allows you to manage taxes more efficiently. For example, knowing how much you can withdraw from tax-deferred accounts like a 401(k), or whether you should convert some of your savings to a Roth IRA to avoid tax penalties in retirement, can help you minimize your tax burden.
12. **Maximizes the use of Social Security and other benefits:** Properly budgeting for retirement allows you to better plan the timing of your Social Security benefits. For example, delaying your benefits until full retirement age or beyond can increase your monthly payout. Budgeting helps you decide when the right time is to start receiving these benefits based on your personal financial situation.

We know this is a lot to consider. One shortcut that can also be helpful is the following budgeting rule of thumb for retirement. Think about any income you might receive on a monthly basis and divide it this way:

- 50 percent needs (essentials like housing, health care, food)
- 30 percent wants (entertainment, hobbies, dining out)
- 20 percent savings/contingency (emergency fund, long-term care)

—Exercise—

Your Retirement Budget

Take a deep breath. Ready? It's time for you to start your own retirement budget. Use the expanded sections on the following pages to build a retirement budget that is customized for your situation. Do some research. Add in exact amounts where possible for completion; if you don't have them, rely on your best estimate to feel in better control of what to expect.

Sources of Income

- **Social Security:** Know what you'll receive and when. Factor in whether you plan to take benefits early or wait for a higher payout.
- **Pensions or annuities:** Consider whether you have guaranteed income sources and how they fit into your budget.
- **Investments:** Decide how much you'll withdraw from your retirement savings (e.g., 401(k), IRAs, or other investment accounts). Consider using the "4 percent rule"—a common guideline that suggests withdrawing 4 percent of your retirement savings annually. (This can vary based on market conditions, inflation, and your personal situation.)
- **Part-time work or business:** If you plan to continue working or have rental income, this should be part of your income estimation.

____

____

____

____

____

____

____

____

Expenses

- **Fixed costs (essentials):** These are nonnegotiable expenses, such as housing (e.g., mortgage, rent), utilities, insurance premiums, transportation (e.g., car payments, public transportation), groceries, clothing, and health care.
- **Variable costs:** These include things like entertainment, travel, luxury goods, home renovations, and other discretionary spending.
- **Unexpected costs:** Build in a buffer for things like home repairs, medical expenses, and other unplanned emergencies.
- **Debt repayment:** Try to enter retirement with as little debt as possible. Paying off any high-interest debt before retirement will ease financial stress.

Health Care Costs

- **Medicare:** While Medicare may cover much of your health care, there are still costs like premiums, copays, and deductibles.
- **Supplemental insurance:** Consider whether you need additional coverage through a Medigap plan or other supplemental insurance, especially for long-term care needs.

- **Long-term care:** As you age, you may need help with daily activities (e.g., nursing homes or in-home care). Budget for this potential need through either savings or long-term care insurance.

Inflation

Inflation will erode your purchasing power over time, so it's important to plan for rising costs, especially in health care, utilities, and food. A good general rule is to add 2–3 percent inflation to your annual budget to help keep up with price increases.

Emergency Fund

Even in retirement, unexpected costs will arise, so it's essential to maintain an emergency fund. Ideally, this should cover three to six months' worth of expenses. A separate emergency fund will help you avoid dipping into your retirement savings if something unexpected comes up.

Withdrawal Strategy

Decide how you will withdraw from your savings. The 4 percent rule is a common guideline. You may also want to create a mix of tax-deferred and taxable accounts to help reduce your tax burden in retirement.

Flexibility

Consider how your lifestyle might change. Do you plan to travel, pick up new hobbies, or spend more on leisure? Factor this into your discretionary spending. It's important to be flexible. As retirement progresses, your needs and wants might change, and your budget should adapt accordingly.

Taxes

Don't forget about taxes! Certain retirement income (e.g., withdrawals from a traditional 401(k) or IRA) will be taxable. Make sure to account for taxes when calculating your withdrawal needs.

Debt-Free Living

Ideally, aim to enter retirement with little or no debt. Paying down your mortgage, credit cards, and other loans before you retire will help reduce your monthly expenses and free up money for other needs.

Retirement Number

Calculate how much money you'll need to sustain your lifestyle in retirement. This *retirement number* is based on your desired monthly expenses, your expected income, and how long you expect to live. If you need help calculating this, tools like retirement calculators can give you a rough estimate. (You can find these on a variety of websites, such as Vanguard or Fidelity.)

Value and Abundance

While we've focused on the practicality of money and how beliefs shape the way you earn and spend, there's another important aspect to consider when it comes to retirement years. Over my years as a therapist, I (Margaret) have observed how often people approach money from a place of restriction or insufficiency. Many don't feel or believe they have enough—no matter how much they actually have. The reassuring sensation of *I have enough* isn't tied to the balance in an IRA or mutual fund; it's a mindset.

No two people share the exact same idea of what having "enough" means. I laughed with a colleague who shared the story of her extremely wealthy client, worried he wouldn't be able to buy his grandson a polo pony if he retired. I joked that I hope I can buy my grandson both popcorn *and* candy when we go to a movie. Abundance looks different to different people.

I had to embrace a new definition of "enough" when I decided to retire. My sense of abundance was based on the belief that as long as I kept working, there would always be enough. But when I transitioned to living on what I had saved, I had to shift that mindset to match my new reality.

The concept of abundance as a mindset was introduced by Stephen Covey in his 1989 book *The 7 Habits of Highly Effective People*. He defined *abundance* as having unlimited resources and the belief that there is more than enough to go around. A key component of contentment is knowing that you have enough. An abundance mindset extends this belief, adding that there's enough for others to have their needs met, too.

Scarcity, on the other hand, is the opposite of abundance and often links to selfishness. It's the zero-sum mindset that if someone else gets something, there won't be enough left for you. It's also the fear of scarcity in retirement—thinking that once you stop earning, you'll never have enough. It's realistic thinking that money could run out during retirement, and some may struggle to meet basic needs. However, once you meet the needs in Maslow's hierarchy, what constitutes "enough" is more based on your expectations.

Planning for a contented retirement involves understanding what's most important to you and adjusting your expectations to fit your budget. Contentment isn't about being able to do everything you want; it's about having reasonable and feasible expectations for your retirement budget. The proverb "You can have anything you want—you just cannot have everything you want" is not a statement of scarcity. It's actually a great clue for how to be content, so you can say, *I do have what I want*. The spiritual corollary is to "want what you have."

—*Exercise*—

What Is Enough?

Allow yourself a few moments for each of the sections in this exercise. See what you have expected will occur in retirement, and how you think and feel about the following from a perspective of abundance:

Your home: Will you stay where you are? Will there be changes in your living situation? Will you spend (more) time at a vacation home? Do you want to downsize?

Downsizing: Are you downsizing from scarcity or abundance? Is there a fear of running out of money? Are you downsizing to maximize your discretionary income? Are you downsizing to decrease time or money on maintenance or to maximize your available time for leisure?

Transition: Even though it may be a decision for the future, have you planned for how you will live when you cannot keep up in your current circumstances? What will this look like? Will you be contented when you achieve that?

Day-to-day activities: What level of social activity interests you? If you are going to belong to clubs or do regular activities that have significant cost, how long do you see yourself doing these? If you enjoy your club or group activities such as gardening, playing Mahjong, going to book club, needleworking, or meditating—do you see yourself doing these activities until ill health stops you? Are these activities affordable?

Mobility: Will you want to travel or vacation? What type of travel appeals to you? What is your expectation about fulfilling your desires based on the costs involved? How much travel will be enough to feel content?

RETIREMENT JOURNAL

Daydreams

Take some time to further absorb the ideas we have presented and move them forward into your retirement thinking by writing in your retirement journal. Allow yourself to have a daydream or image of what you want and wish for:

- If you could have anything you want when you are retired, what would that be?
- What is most important to you in retirement to feel that you have an abundant life?
- What does "enough" mean to you?

Shifting from Fear to Love

As you read through this chapter and complete the exercises and journal prompts, you may still feel scared to think through your retirement financial needs. Money can have that effect on any of us, because it is the source of so much global anxiety. The anxiety or fear that money imparts is often due to the following:

- **Lack of financial literacy:** Few of us were taught how to manage money properly. Without the necessary skills or knowledge to handle finances, it can feel overwhelming to make the "right" decisions; this can cause fear of making mistakes or facing consequences.
- **Social pressure:** Society often places a lot of emphasis on financial success and wealth, which can make us feel inadequate or like we're falling behind if we don't have a lot of money. The fear of judgment or feeling "less than" can make dealing with money more stressful.
- **Fear of loss or scarcity:** Money represents security and survival to many people, and the fear of losing it can trigger anxiety. If we have had negative experiences with money, such as going into debt, losing a job, or facing financial instability, it can create a lasting fear of money.
- **Emotional attachment:** Money is often tied to personal emotions, like stress, guilt, or even shame. You may have complex feelings about money based on your upbringing, cultural views, or personal experiences. For example, you may feel guilty about spending money on yourself or fear being seen as greedy.

- **Uncertainty and the unknown:** Financial decisions often come with uncertainty, such as investments, savings, or taxes. The fear of not knowing what will happen, or making a decision that leads to financial instability, can paralyze you into avoiding money-related tasks altogether.
- **Inaccessibility:** For some, finances can feel like a world that's difficult to enter or understand. Whether it's a lack of access to financial advice, complicated language around money, or systemic barriers like income inequality, the world of finance can seem intimidating and out of reach.

You can shift from fear to love in all areas of life, including how you relate to money. Use the previous list to help identify steps you can take and resources that will make you feel stronger and more secure. In the workshops I (Lynn) have led as a business coach for therapists over the past thirty years, I end each presentation by focusing on the concept of shifting from fear to love. This involves addressing anything we resist or feel frightened by, but know we must take action on to move forward. I ask those in my workshops to think about this simple but evocative definition from writer Neale Donald Walsch (1996, p.19), clarifying the difference between fear and love:

> *Fear is the energy which contracts, closes down, draws in, runs, hides, hoards, harms.*
>
> *Love is the energy which expands, opens up, sends out, stays, reveals, shares, heals.*
>
> *Fear holds close, love holds dear.*
>
> *Fear grasps, love lets go.*

If you find yourself closing down or feeling small as you move forward with your financial planning for retirement, take a moment to pause. Sit up straight and allow your body to expand. Stretch your arms overhead or stand tall. Take a deep breath.

Notice any signs of fear in your body or mind. Try to stay open and curious to all possibilities. Slow down. Reread your data. Approach it with a fresh, open mind.

Let go of cognitive distortions—those automatic "shoulds," "always," or "nevers." If you're feeling stuck, shift your environment. Take a walk. Step outside. Find a space in nature that offers you perspective.

Soothe yourself first—then return to your planning, grounded and clear.

Find ways to bring a sense of love and ease into your financial planning: Listen to music as you do your budget. Remember your love for your profession and your desire to end it well. Extend your budget to include a love of self and family and a desire to have those you care for be secure and independent. Validate yourself for all your efforts and meaningful work, and accept the rewards and true abundance that retirement can offer.

RETIREMENT JOURNAL

Fear to Love

Reflect on the following prompts in your retirement journal to uncover any additional fear you might still have as you further consider financial planning:

- What energy in you is closing down? How can you expand and open up?
- Where do you feel yourself being on the run, hiding, or hoarding as you try to plan financially? How can you stay calm, reveal, and heal?
- What are you holding too close? How can you hold dear and let go?
- How can you extend love to yourself and others as you work through the process of preparing for financial responsibility?
- What does it mean if you attend to this task from a place of love instead of fear?
- What else do you need in order to feel calm and secure when addressing your finances? Who can help you? How will you find support to complete this budgeting task?

Moving Forward

Now, we move into the fourth and final stage of the Readiness for Retirement Model—Stage IV: Action: A New Beginning. This stage is about looking ahead, understanding what's next in your journey as you claim your legacy, and reflecting on all you've achieved and the lives you've impacted throughout your career.

This next section is designed to help you embrace retirement with positivity, enthusiasm, and an open heart so you can fully appreciate all that this new chapter of your life has to offer. It's a time to celebrate your accomplishments while also embracing the exciting possibilities that lie ahead.

Stage IV

Action: A New Beginning

The fourth stage of the Readiness for Retirement Model is not only about the process of walking away from your career with appreciation for all you have achieved; it's also about understanding what you are walking toward. A well-rounded plan involves recognizing what you take with you—your legacy—and how it will serve you in the future.

In this final stage, we help you reflect on your accomplishments and claim your legacy, an aspect often underestimated by many therapists. Recognizing all that you have done and the ripple effect of your work can provide a sense of satisfaction and ease in letting go. We also explore the new identity you may adopt in retirement, which can open new doors and opportunities. Finally, we help you envision your future with a sense of potential, curiosity, and excitement.

The chapters in the action stage can serve as a springboard, igniting engagement and optimism about your future.

—Chapter 10—

Legacy: Knowing Your Worth, Remembering Your Impact

As therapists, we don't expect our clients to throw us a retirement party. If you've spent years in private practice, you know there won't be gold watches, balloons, or cakes marking your departure after decades of service. And yet, if there were, it might be easier to see what you've built, understand how you've affected others, and feel more certain of your impact and value.

Retirees in other professions receive awards, plaques, and even medals that show the appreciation of their colleagues, often accompanied by a long review of their contributions. People can leave a workplace knowing how others have appreciated their contributions. If you are a therapist working in an agency or a public or private organization, you might be celebrated this way by your colleagues, but the people you directly helped—your clients—won't be part of that.

When retiring, it's natural to want to know that your work has made a difference and held meaning. Being able to say to yourself, *Well done, I did enough!* can help and provide some satisfaction. But how do you decide if you've done enough?

A therapist's efforts are not always observable outside of the office. Our relationships with clients are real and often profound, but they remain confidential. Our work is typically one-directional: We attend to the client in a private setting without others observing. This confidentiality limits our ability to receive feedback about our clients' progress from others, to observe them in their social world, or to hear from family and friends about the changes they make.

We are one of the few professions that does not ask clients to fill out public satisfaction surveys or post five-star reviews. Unlike the continuous feedback culture we see today—where businesses ask for "likes" on everything from fast-food purchases to consulting a neurosurgeon—therapy operates differently. We cannot post client reviews on our websites because we do not reveal the identities of those we see. Nor can we ask clients to post reviews, as doing so would fundamentally alter the nature of our relationship with them.

The private nature of our work relies on discretion to maintain the safe haven we create for each client. Clients trust their therapists to keep their sessions confidential. This trust allows them to explore personal challenges, share successes and setbacks, heal from trauma, and become vulnerable enough to reveal their true emotional and mental states. Moreover, clients rely on the wisdom of their therapists to help them set meaningful goals, learn strategies for improvement, and process their feelings about the progress they make on that journey.

We notice our clients' courage and progress. We see their efforts to keep trying, to be honest with themselves, to accept themselves and live more authentically—but we observe this without an audience. No one else may ever know what hard work has gone into that process of change. For our part, we bring to bear our years of gradually developed expertise to be of help. That, too, is work. And we delight in seeing it pay off. We also know—and we may be the only ones who know—that when we are fully engaged with our clients, we invest tremendous energy, emotion, and thoughtful reflection on the needs of those clients.

In this chapter, we help you to reflect on your accomplishments and assess your legacy. Ultimately, you alone may be the one who shapes your understanding of the impact you've had on the world. As retirement nears, taking time to consider your contributions and evaluate your legacy can help you recognize your value to the individuals, teams, and communities you've served.

Have You Done Enough?

At times, we may feel as though we haven't worked as hard because psychotherapy doesn't require physical stamina in the same way many other jobs do. We don't need to lift heavy objects or remain on our feet all day. Unless cognitive decline changes things, we can continue to listen, assess, learn, and share our wisdom with clients well past the typical retirement age.

But we expend energy. The human brain utilizes 30 percent of the body's calories in a day. And we are using those brains energetically! Our profession is demanding, even if it doesn't take an obvious toll on our bodies. When we consider stepping away from the work we love, it's essential to reflect on our achievements. Lacking an answer to the question *Have I done enough?* can be an obstacle to retiring. There are two ways to appraise the work you have done.

One way is to list your accomplishments that are measurable. For example:

- You chaired the team that opened the first childhood autism clinic in your town.
- You started a group psychotherapy practice that keeps eight other therapists gainfully employed.

Legacy is the second way to evaluate your broader impact:

- In that autism clinic, the children whom you helped could utilize their talents and contribute to their communities.
- Your legacy as a business owner employing therapists is the ongoing value that high-quality mental health care brings to your community.

The ongoing benefit others take from your accomplishments defines your legacy.

Imagine that you helped a client overcome depression. As a result, they become a better spouse and gain the energy to excel in their nonprofit work. Their team grows more cohesive and the community benefits. In this case, you've accomplished an important therapeutic goal. The legacy of your work extends far beyond the individual.

Similarly, when you help another client heal from trauma, you achieve the objectives of therapy and resolve the trauma. But in doing so, you break a generational cycle of abuse, and your legacy becomes the long-term impact on future generations. The legacy of your work—session by session, day by day—can touch countless others, often in ways that are difficult to measure.

As therapists, the legacy of our work is a gift that keeps on giving. And that's worth thinking about.

Our work doesn't always lend itself to measuring success or outcomes in the same way other professions do, and it's possible you've never tried to calculate your impact. This is why the question of legacy becomes so crucial when it's time to say goodbye to the work you love. Reflecting on and then enumerating the key aspects of your work can help you recognize the far-reaching influence you've had on your community.

Use the following exercise to help you enumerate your accomplishments and assess your legacy. Identifying what you have accomplished and how it becomes your legacy can both help you to answer the questions *Have I made a difference? Did I do enough?*

—Exercise—

Your Legacy

This exercise will ask you to estimate numbers. Do not attempt to go back over a long career to research exact numbers. The point here is *not* the specific count, but instead to recognize the broad scope of what you have contributed. If you get caught on exact numbers, you might fall into the trap of comparison with others—the exceptionalism trap.

Take a moment before you begin to quickly answer this deliberately vague and very subjective first question:

1. On a scale of 1–100, with 1 being "Not at all" and 100 being "Totally," how satisfied are you today with how much you have accomplished in your career? ______________

As you consider the answers to the next section of questions, just estimate. There is no need to exactly document them. Please make notes to yourself as you remember specific individuals or groups or jobs. Answer the following:

2. Estimate the number of clients you have seen over all the years of your work. (This is your accomplishment.) ______________
3. Multiply that number by 10 for the people those clients had an impact on. This is a solid guess on how many people you have also influenced by seeing your clients. (This is your legacy.) ______________
   a. Do you feel especially proud regarding the work you did for any specific clients?

      ____

      ____
4. How many people have you supervised? (Accomplishment) ______
5. How many courses have you taught? (Accomplishment) ________

6. How many lectures have you given? (Accomplishment) __________

7. How many students have you taught? (Accomplishment) ________

    a. Will the people you taught, mentored, or supervised go on to be better in their careers because of your work together? (Legacy)

    ____

    ____

    b. Now reflect. How many people might those students have had a positive impact on? Your work is multiplied in their use of your wisdom, especially if they worked in the field, as you did. Multiply the number of students by 10. (Legacy) ____________

8. What contributions during your career make you feel proud or positive about your work? Did you work with a challenging population that others may have found difficult to work with? Did you do something unique? (Accomplishment)

    ____

    ____

    a. What do you think the legacy of that accomplishment will be?

    ____

    ____

9. How many articles, books, or curricula have you written? (Accomplishment) ______________________________

    a. Do you have an idea of how many books were sold or how many people read your articles? (Legacy) ________________

    b. Have you written a blog? Can you estimate how many people read it? Have you received positive feedback? (Your legacy is how they use that information, and how they share it.)

    ____

    ____

10. Do you have a social media presence related to your work? (Posting is an accomplishment. The number of followers and people sharing the posts is your legacy.) How many followers do you have? ________

    a. How have you used that to further your career? (Accomplishment)

    ____

    ____

    b. How have you used that to promote mental health well-being in the community? (Legacy)

    ____

    ____

11. What organizations have you contributed to? (Accomplishment)

    ____

    ____

    a. How have you advanced the profession through participation or attendance at meetings, conferences, or trainings for those organizations? (Legacy)

    ____

    ____

    b. What programs, organizations, or groups that you helped develop will continue after you leave? (Legacy)

    ____

    ____

12. Who did you help informally, such as friends, family, or colleagues, using your skills outside of the professional arena?

    ____

    ____

a. In what ways did they go on to apply your help? (Their impact on others is part of your legacy.)

____

____

Now rethink the answer to the earlier question:

13. On a scale of 1–100, with 1 being "Not at all" and 100 being "Totally," how satisfied are you today with how much you have accomplished in your career? ____________________

14. How has filling out this legacy questionnaire affected you? Start with five minutes of writing. Make your answer a stream of consciousness; do not worry about making it sound perfect. You can return to it later.

____

____

____

____

____

____

15. What did you wish to do that you haven't yet done in your career?

____

____

16. How will you work to make that happen? If you cannot do more or do not wish to, how will you reconcile yourself to the reality of an unmet goal?

____

____

As you are moving toward envisioning your future, keep your legacy exercise handy. It will reassure you that you are, in fact, enough.

When Is It Time?

Now you have a clearer sense of what you've accomplished and the legacy you've created. You've honed valuable skills and put them to great use, making a meaningful difference in people's lives. For some of us, though, the very impact we've had can make it harder to know when to step away. We therapists often need time to grow into our careers. It takes time to age in, and aging out is not an easy transition.

Developing expertise takes time. Think back to your early therapy training, when you likely experimented with new methods and concepts to see what resonated best with your clients. The more you applied different techniques and tested out theories, the more you learned and refined your approach. In the early years of your career, you probably explored many options, trying to find what worked best.

These early years were filled with experimentation: What did you enjoy doing? What were you good at? What engaged your intellect, and what new ideas sparked your interest? Like most therapists, you honed your skills, discovered your preferred methods, and became more comfortable with certain approaches. This developmental stage involved testing out the techniques you learned in training, but it also likely included finding your own creative solutions to meet client needs. Perhaps you even developed some innovative approaches.

For new therapists in training, the process of learning often involves fitting techniques to their personal style, guided by their preferences and the needs of their clients. They are energized by new information and fueled by the cyclical process of learning, trying, and refining—a pattern that defines the early years of their career.

These early years of experimentation lead to the development of new theories and techniques. Some of these ideas catch the attention of peers and become major contributions to the field. Consider, for example, Francine Shapiro's development of eye movement desensitization and reprocessing (EMDR) or Sue Johnson's work with emotionally focused therapy, among many others. Their breakthroughs in client treatment were fueled by creative energy—the kind more typical of younger, energetic therapists who are willing to take risks and share ideas with their peers. It takes this specific energy, this stage of developing and experimenting, to achieve such advancements.

As you progress in your career, you begin to build a solid knowledge base. Gaining confidence and feeling like an expert in your work takes time, as you must accumulate understanding not only about your methods but also about when and how to apply them. You learn how clients respond to your approach and adjust your techniques to meet their individual needs. While therapists continue learning and evolving throughout their careers, as they gain experience, they integrate that knowledge from a place of confidence in their knowledge and expertise.

This is why it takes time to get good at the process of therapy. No wonder newer therapists tend to feel overwhelmed for a long time after coming into the profession. As one student therapist questioned, "At what age will I feel as if I know what I am doing? When will I feel confident?"

Think about how a musician learns, practicing skills until playing the instrument becomes a pattern without conscious intention. When attention is freed from technique, the musician can develop a style of playing, one that expresses their musical preference. Once they master their instrument, they can capture nuance in a piece and alter it at will to suit the moment. Our youngest musicians might produce the most creative new music, but elder musicians can play with confidence and deep expressiveness. You only have to think of the therapists you admire to see how this mirrors career development in our profession. Our master therapists become our wisest teachers, sharing their knowledge in classrooms and trainings and helping other therapists apply their theory or techniques in the real world of psychotherapy.

Over time and with practice, therapists accumulate knowledge and settle into patterns that produce results, increasing not only confidence but wisdom—when and how to apply what we know. This is what we mean by "aging into" our careers. When you are an elder in this profession, you can be filled with a quiet confidence and a deep, earned sense of knowing, and it can be hard to step away from doing therapy once you feel you have fully developed—or even mastered—your craft.

RETIREMENT JOURNAL

Earned Knowledge

Describe the methodologies and perspectives that grabbed your attention in your first ten years in the field by considering the following prompts in your retirement journal:

- Did these relate to each other or build on each other?
- Did you sample varied styles of working or explore theories that fit different clientele or workplaces?
- What happened to your knowledge base in the middle of your career?
- What happened to your knowledge base in your late career?
- How confident do you feel about the work you do?

Your Legacy If You Started Later in Life

Another reason it's hard to "age out" of our profession is that some of us enter therapy as a second career. Women, in particular, may begin working later, having paused or delayed their careers to care for young children. For these individuals, the learn-try-learn-repeat pattern of training often starts in their midforties, without a specific background in their area of interest. While they bring valuable life wisdom that helps them absorb and apply new information, the confidence that comes from accumulated knowledge and experience in psychotherapy may not fully develop until their late fifties.

The student therapist mentioned earlier—the one who asked how old she would be when she felt confident—entered the field after her children had left home. She was forty-five; she may not feel secure in her craft until she reaches her late fifties. For second-career therapists, hitting their stride in their late fifties or early sixties, the prospect of retirement can feel especially difficult. By this point, they've gained confidence in their skills, and while others around them may be discussing their imminent retirement, they still feel ready to keep working. They're eager to embrace their expertise and enjoy the certainty they've earned over the years.

However, we must acknowledge that age brings inevitable changes we can't ignore. Around the age of seventy, most of us will begin to experience some decline. At the very least, our mental energy will start to diminish, whether gradually or more suddenly. Preparing to step away from the work we love needs to happen before serious decline sets in, because once it does, it may become difficult to evaluate when and how it's best to retire.

RETIREMENT JOURNAL

Hitting Your Stride

Use the following prompts to reflect on your growth and development as a therapist:

- At what age did you begin your career as a psychotherapist?
- At what point did you "hit your stride"?
- Was there a specific time or position in your career that signified to you that you "now know what you are doing"?
- Do you notice a difference in your confidence related to different aspects of your work?
- How does it feel to reach your peak or find your rhythm and then decide to retire?

Leaving on a High Note

Western culture, and the United States in particular, places a premium on exceptionalism. We celebrate the GOAT (Greatest of All Time) in sports, or the EGOT (Emmy, Grammy, Oscar, Tony) winners in TV, music, stage, and film—titles that reflect careers built on talent, effort, and discipline. These are well-deserved achievements. We can point to individuals whose early successes continue as their talents mature, and we often see their experience reflected in their evolving careers as they age. Some even use their success to fuel a new level of contribution to society.

One inspiring example of this is Andre Agassi, the exceptional tennis star who has devoted himself to education. Nearing the end of his tennis career, he founded a school in Las Vegas in 2001 to serve underserved youth, creating a model for how to provide meaningful education to those who need it most early in life. Agassi was truly exceptional in tennis; now, as an older man, he has successfully transitioned into a career that is entirely different from the one of his youth, applying the same discipline, commitment, and abilities.

However, our culture is also filled with celebrities of questionable abilities—individuals whose societal value is often defined by the number of followers they have on social media. These so-called influencers often have little knowledge, experience, or training to justify their popularity. They simply captured the attention of users on media platforms. While they may have amassed extraordinary followings, they are not necessarily exceptional talents, workers, or even people. At best, they are lucky.

The allure of Instagram, X (formerly Twitter), and TikTok lies in the possibility of "going viral"—reaching an audience whose exceptional size would be nearly impossible in a real-world community, where interactions are more limited and personal. This allure has driven many people to compulsively post on various platforms, often in search of fame, but rarely with the intention of contributing something meaningful to society. Our culture seems to abhor ordinariness. But if you can't tolerate being ordinary, how can you ever approach true satisfaction?

It might be hard to accept, but most of us ordinary people are not exceptional. This does not mean we are not unique, valuable, or worthwhile. In a culture of exceptionalism, it's not always easy to recognize that we are enough. We can live rich lives full of meaning and purpose without ever receiving awards or public recognition for our work. We can learn to be satisfied with our achievements and our legacy.

The decision to retire often comes when we reach a point in our hearts, minds, and lives where we can say something like "I have done enough. I am ready to move on. I've given all I can, fulfilled my role, and completed my work." This realization comes at different stages for everyone. Since there are so many ways to approach our work and countless forms of psychotherapy, there is no single, clear-cut definition of what "enough" looks like. While the *Your Legacy* worksheet is one helpful tool to answer that question, another is assessing your value within yourself and within your circle of influence. Achieving fame is not necessary to leave a legacy of true value.

Your career has likely followed a steady, gradual trajectory rather than a path to stardom. As you approach retirement, it's important to recognize that the consistent progress you've made over the years holds significant value. This steady achievement is a testament to the impact you've had, even if it wasn't always in the spotlight.

It's not necessary to have a visibly outstanding career to feel satisfied. Many individuals who experience significant success early in their careers struggle to accept their declining abilities as they age, especially when they can no longer sustain that level of achievement. The most obvious examples are sports stars who can no longer perform at their peak. They may retire after a championship season, looking back on it as a high point. As an older therapist, however, you don't have a "championship game" experience to mark an ending, and you may well still feel confident in your skills. Although you might find it hard to accept, it can be best for you and your clients if you leave while you are working well rather than waiting until you notice your decline.

Pinpointing the right time to leave can be complicated because your success has been built on steady, reliable work over months and years, not a single dramatic achievement with one client, akin to taking home a trophy. But, like boxers who keep returning to the ring for one last shot at a title, staying in the job while knowing you're no longer at your best diminishes your ability to feel your true value.

Leave on a high note. It's much harder to feel true satisfaction in your accomplishments and legacy if you're in decline and leave on a low note. We want you to recognize your full value so you can choose the optimal time to step away.

Moving Forward

The transition from outward-focused energy of developing a career to deeper reflection about legacy may happen at different points in life, influenced by lifestyle factors like the age at which you started a family or began your career. By assessing your accomplishments and legacy and reflecting on the right time to retire on a high note, you'll be better prepared to make that shift and take action when the time is right.

Having reflected on your career, it is time to consider what will now bring satisfaction and even new growth in a different direction once you retire. In our next two chapters, we will offer ideas for how to envision this next stage of life.

—Chapter 11—

Your Retirement Integrity

Joanna had a wide-ranging career. She started as a social worker in a mental health clinic, then became a hospital chaplain, and later worked for a nonprofit organization focused on integrating immigrant families into the community. When that agency lost its funding, she was forced into retirement. Now sixty-nine and seven years removed from the workforce, she reflects on her career.

"The hardest part of being forced into retirement was losing my sense of purpose," she said. "I was always a woman who served. Now, I'm not."

In retirement, Joanna wandered without direction, dabbling in activities that had once interested her but now felt disconnected from her identity. "I've always been committed to helping others. That's what gave my life meaning. Without the service opportunities that defined my career and my worth, I feel adrift."

When your work is centered on meaning and purpose, what draws you into retirement? For many therapists who view their profession as a vocation rather than just a job, finding activities that provide a similar sense of purpose is crucial to making a successful transition. However, the kinds of activities that feel meaningful can differ greatly from person to person. It takes time to reflect on what will be significant in this new chapter of life.

A Life of Purpose

While living a life filled with meaning and purpose is desirable at every stage, what makes life feel purposeful evolves over time (Vaillant, 2003). As baby boomers have entered retirement, the concept of "successful aging" has gained prominence, often defined by the ability to maintain high levels of emotional resilience and physical function (Blasco-Belled & Alsinet, 2022; Buettner, 2017). Studies on happiness and well-being in older adults, particularly those over the age of seventy, emphasize the critical role of feeling useful and valuable in maintaining both health and emotional balance (Krause, 2004; Ryff & Keyes, 1995; Taylor & Brown, 1988).

How one is useful may vary considerably, but *believing* one is useful is the key.

In retirement, Joanna no longer believed she served a purpose. Though she engaged in various activities meant to enrich her new life, she was surprised to find that they didn't provide the satisfaction she had hoped for. Volunteering and activism—things she thought would replace the sense of purpose and importance she had felt in her career—left her feeling disappointed. These activities lacked the intensity and impact of her former work, leaving her drained rather than fulfilled.

Joanna struggled with discouragement and began to lose her optimism about the future. She had been abruptly disconnected from her role of service, and the sense of incompleteness that followed led her to feel unproductive—a state foreign to her. This feeling of disconnection from society only deepened her sense of isolation.

Believing that your life has meaning and purpose in retirement can significantly improve your outlook as well as help you to maintain physical mobility and intellectual acuity in later years. (Pull factors toward retirement, discussed in chapter 1, may include a variety of activities, such as volunteering, spending time with family, providing social support to others, and other pursuits that enhance well-being.) However, like Joanna, many people find that retirement is not always a smooth or immediate transition. It's often not possible to simply replicate the feelings and sense of purpose from your therapy career within retirement activities. Instead, you may need to experiment and explore different paths to discover what truly fits your needs and interests.

Understanding the developmental stages of life, and how the transition into retirement shifts us from one stage to the next, can be a helpful step in navigating this change.

Defining Retirement Integrity

Erik Erikson (1994), in his work on the eight developmental stages of life, described a progression of awareness and acceptance in aging that emphasizes the importance of contributing to society and guiding the next generation. This can be done through parenting, work, or community involvement. Erikson suggests that when individuals feel connected to society and perceive themselves as contributing to its well-being, they successfully fulfill this seventh stage of development—"Generativity versus Stagnation."

"Integrity versus Despair" is the eighth and final stage of Erikson's theory of psychosocial development, occurring during late adulthood (typically around age sixty-five and beyond). This stage centers on how individuals reflect on their lives as they approach the end. *Integrity* refers to the point at which people look back and feel a sense of fulfillment, pride in their accomplishments, and overall contentment. They recognize that their lives have had meaning and made a positive impact, and they feel at peace with the legacy they will leave behind. This sense of integrity brings wisdom and acceptance of their life's journey.

In the context of retirement, feeling integrity and wholeness means finding ways to stay connected to a sense of purpose even after professional or caregiving roles have ended. As people age, they often reflect on their careers, relationships, and accomplishments. Those who find meaning in their past experiences and continue to contribute to the well-being of others—through activities like volunteering or mentoring—are more likely to experience a greater sense of integrity and wholeness.

Becoming a sage celebrates the culmination of your life's experiences. Wisdom seems inherently connected to becoming more peaceful and making choices that enrich us. How you use that wisdom in the arenas of your retired life is an important choice. It will continue to reinforce your identity as a person who contributed and is still valuable.

We need to update Erikson's theories to reflect our population's longer lifespan. Many people continue to live energetically well past age sixty-five and still have aspirations they want to pursue beyond their careers. For many therapists, retirement offers the opportunity to engage in new work or pursue goals that were previously put on hold due to the demands of earning a living. However, before retiring, it's crucial to explore and evaluate which activities will best align with our sense of self and support our ambitions for the years ahead. This process of exploration can make all the difference in retiring well and living meaningfully.

As one of our interviewees, Marilee, remarked, "I find I can fulfill the same goals that caused me to start out in my career, the goals of helping other people. Now I can do this as an activist for climate change, helping the larger community—not just helping one person at a time." Her identity will be intact through her retirement and contribute to her later years' sense of integrity about her life.

Arthur C. Brooks (2024), in an article about happiness for *The Atlantic*, commented that all people find it hard to step back when they have a professional identity of which they feel proud. That reluctance persists despite the reasoning part of their brain telling them it would be wise to retire at the top of their game. Accomplished men in particular are at risk for depression when they retire, primarily due to stepping away from power, from the trappings of the job that gave them worth and meaning. They find it difficult to replace such heady rewards for their ego and status.

Brooks's remarks strike a chord for psychotherapists. For us, the trappings are not typically public acclaim or recognition, but are more subtle, like the daily validation of our sessions with clients showing progress. We may have status from positions on boards for various organizations, or establishing an office and staff where we still delight to work, but those jobs are ultimately all in the service of client care. You might not be stepping away from power as much of the world defines it, but you definitely will be stepping away from a role in which you felt valuable and worthwhile.

RETIREMENT JOURNAL

Stages of Retirement Integrity

We have asked you to do this kind of review about your career in several different ways before, but in this entry in your retirement journal, we suggest taking a slightly different tack: How do you see yourself in Erikson's last stage of integrity or wholeness as it relates to the life you have lived?

- Have you come to terms with your past, including successes and failures?
- Do you feel peace of mind, contentment, and wisdom, acknowledging that your life has had meaning?
- Do you have any regrets?
- Have you lived in alignment with your values, even if you made some mistakes?

Appreciating Your Clinical House

Saying goodbye to both people and things is a deeply complex process. When I (Lynn) moved out of the first house I owned, I became acutely aware of all that the house represented and all the memories it held. There were so many "firsts" tied to it: the first kitchen where I taught myself to cook, the first dining room filled with cast-off furniture that was gratefully received, my son's first bedroom decorated with rock-star posters, and my first attempt at gardening in the small plot behind the house. I walked from room to room, space to space, recalling the key moments that had unfolded in each area.

After shedding tears and expressing gratitude, thanking the house for its shelter and stability, I was finally ready to hand over the keys to the new owner. Since then, I've lived in other homes, but I repeat this process each time I leave—honoring not just who I was in the space, but how the space itself often shaped me.

Just as selling a house or moving from one apartment to another involves leaving behind a space that once served you, your clinical space evolves over the course of your career. Take a moment to reflect on all that you did within your clinical "house"—the literal or metaphorical spaces that held your work. Saying goodbye to these spaces goes beyond simply assessing your legacy, as you did in chapter 10. Allow yourself to truly say farewell and appreciate the arc of your career as you prepare to embrace the new.

RETIREMENT JOURNAL

A Final Walkthrough of Your Clinical House

When you leave a home or an apartment, you do a final walkthrough to see if there are any things left behind, or just to remember the space. Call on this imagery to close the door on a career as you answer the prompts in your retirement journal.

As you read the prompts, visualize yourself walking through the offices, rooms, or buildings where you practiced your craft, mentally revisiting the environments that housed your efforts. Envision those who inhabited those rooms with you, remembering colleagues, particular clients, or clinical contributions you made. Think about why you moved from each room to the next. We suggest you go deep into your memory, finding the flavor, tone, and ambience of the place or time in your life. You may pause to close your eyes, remember the music of the time, see the physical surroundings, and visualize yourself as you were.

It might work best for you to just visualize all the prompts first and write when you are done; alternatively, you could write after "leaving each room."

- **Your first internship or job:** What were your responsibilities? Who was your supervisor? What kinds of clients did you have? Who were your colleagues? What did you learn? How did this affect your career direction? What prompted you to move on?
- **Your next assignment:** How did you determine your next step? How much was it your choice versus being affected by life circumstances, such as a move, a marriage, or a family event? Was your next step to get more education or additional certification?
- **Your next job:** Did you stay in the same community? What personal events were shaping your career choice? What was your new role? Did you feel as if you were moving forward with more income, more responsibility, and more recognition? Who were your colleagues? Did you develop professional relationships or friendships?
- What kind of changes to your style of work were occurring? Did you learn methodologies that shaped the way you worked? Did you develop new professional relationships that contributed to new learning?
- How did new learning move your work as a psychotherapist to a new or different level of work? What stages of growth, learning, and progress did you go through? Did you experience disappointments along the way? How did your style and method of work develop over time?
- What new aspects of your career did you embrace? Did you develop a group or take on a role in education, leadership, or professional development that expanded your work to larger groups or new demographics?
- As you "came into your own," maturing and finding a clear stylistic path, where did you do the work of your career? Who worked with you and around you? What kind of space were you in? What kind of community were you living and working in? How did that reflect you and your values and achievements?
- How would you describe the clinical seat you occupy at the end of your career?
- As you get ready to walk out of you career home and close the door, is there anything that you still want to do or something you wish you had done (or had time to do) before saying, "This is enough"?
- Do you have a date in mind when you will officially or formally retire?

Discovering New Depths

After feeling dispirited in her search for meaningful activities in retirement, Joanna had a revelation. While she had spent time dabbling in one activity after another, all of which she eventually abandoned, something new had quietly emerged. She had become deeply engaged in her garden, studying organic methods and learning which plants thrived in her particular environment. She grew plants both for food and, to her surprise, for the pursuit of beauty.

Joanna said, "I feel connected to the environment in a way I have never experienced before."

She described the almost spiritual experience of designing flower beds to attract bees and butterflies and proudly showed a close-up photo of monarchs atop her milkweed. Yard work, which had once been a chore, was now something that engaged her mentally, emotionally, and spiritually. The moment she realized, "I am a gardener," she discovered an identity that resonated deeply with her values. She felt at peace, as if her sense of self had reformed through this new realm of activity that fully met her desire for a meaningful and useful life on a global scale. She was doing service for the earth.

It had taken her years, but in line with Erikson's concept of generativity, she found a new domain in which to live out her values.

Unless you begin to create fulfilling activities that utilize your skills, you may flounder in retirement. Unlike Joanna, who was thrust into a new stage without preparation, you have the advantage from your prior reading, retirement journaling, and exercises for reflection and planning. Rather than being forced into the unknown, you can take time to experiment while still engaged in work that is familiar and meaningful. You can be a gardener of ideas, planting seeds and seeing what grows, or you can be an architect, carefully building a structured retirement plan. By reflecting, observing, and experimenting, you can try out various activities ahead of time, discovering which ones feel right and truly fulfilling.

Your Values and Retirement Choices

Your retirement values and goals will reflect your personality and life experiences and may not necessarily look like another person's. After closing her practice, Sharon reported, "When I retired a year ago, I decided I would only do things I have never done before. I want to explore. There are so many things that interest me that I have had no time for."

When she was asked by the community center to lead a local group for meditation, she declined. The organizer objected, "But you are so good at this—please agree to help us." Sharon politely asked the organizer to find another leader and took off to hike on her own for three months—a lifelong goal impossible to fulfill while employed. As a therapist, she had focused on helping clients with self-care; now, in retirement, she was happily doing the same for herself. Her values about the importance of well-being stayed intact.

Edward was active online, wrote books, and trained therapists. He felt drawn to spend his retirement working with environmental conservation. He stepped away from writing and training and eagerly took up new activities that he had longed to do but had no time for when he was still actively employed. In this new endeavor, he still kept true to his core purpose of caring for others, but he redirected his activities to a cause that deeply moved him at this later stage of life.

Barbara, a psychologist and instructor in mindful meditation, is readying for retirement in the coming year. She emphasized, "I don't want to have *any regular* demands. I have long advocated living mindfully and at a pace that allows one's spirit to grow. I want to see how my life evolves, paying attention to what moves me without having to rush away from something that might be good for me." She values spiritual development and has undertaken to study spiritual traditions of other cultures as well as devote more time to meditation.

Barbara said, "I have never had all the time I wanted to see how a peaceful, meditative life would develop for me. I am open to something new developing, but it feels so good to know I have time to wait and see." She is not stagnating; she is taking her time—not jumping into hectic activity. This meditative life feels potently meaningful to her.

In your post-retirement plans, take your values into consideration. For me (Margaret), being useful is a powerful value, so I want my life to be one in which I continue to be of service. In retirement, I can fulfill that value in so many ways: I drive my grandson to school to save his parents time for their workday, I volunteer for a local organization raising money for women's shelters, and I even spread mulch as a volunteer at a beautiful arboretum. I did none of these things when I was engaged in my career.

There is no one correct way to live out your values. You just need to do this with intention.

RETIREMENT JOURNAL

Intentions and Values

Consider your intentions and values by reflecting on the following prompts in your retirement journal:

- What is it that makes you feel proud of yourself?
- What activities are congruent with your view of yourself?
- What seeds are you planting for your future?
- What are you building for a structured retirement plan?

—*Exercise*—

Your Values

In this exercise, you will make a list of twenty-five words that describe yourself. This list is essentially a snapshot of your values. After you create this list, identify, for each value, one way that you could live out this value (or one way that others would see it in you). If you run out of ideas, ask a friend what they might put on a list of your talents, characteristics, and the values you embody.

Value, Talent, or Characteristic	Activity You Use This In
1.	
2.	
3.	
4.	
5.	
6.	
7.	
8.	
9.	
10.	

Value, Talent, or Characteristic	Activity You Use This In
11.	
12.	
13.	
14.	
15.	
16.	
17.	
18.	
19.	
20.	
21.	
22.	
23.	
24.	
25.	

Relationships in Retirement

Many of us value our families and our friends; in retirement, we can devote more attention to life partners, aging parents, siblings, extended family, and those "chosen family members" that are close friends. Social connections are important throughout our life, but they become vital as we age. Investigating what makes people happy, researchers repeatedly find that relationships are critical for our lifelong happiness (Hitchcott et al., 2018; Olsen et al., 1991).

The global COVID-19 pandemic prompted research about how isolation affected people in every age group, and it was evident that adolescents suffered most during that period. That was not surprising, because we know that deepening social relationship skills is a significant developmental task of this age group. However, the degree to which elders were affected *was* surprising. Rapid cognitive decline was observable in the elderly who were isolated and had very limited contact with others, as was the case in assisted living and nursing facilities. Wanting the elderly to be safe, the protocols for physical health failed to consider how loneliness would affect the quality of the residents' lives and mental health (Ingram et al., 2021).

During this time, it was also true that many people found relief in dropping out of social circles that had *not* been highly rewarding. Eliminating time with casual acquaintances was easy when we had to limit the number of people in our "bubble." It gave many people the opportunity to drift away from relationships that were otherwise not fulfilling. Diminishing social connections by attrition was easy at that time.

Clark, a retired therapist, shared in our survey that much of his prepandemic social time had been spent with people who weren't truly vital to his life. During the pandemic, he made a conscious decision to focus his energy on those whose presence enriched his life or to whom he felt genuinely important. After retiring, he maintained this selectivity—simply letting go of peripheral connections. He found that doing so improved his well-being: He felt less pressure, less annoyance, and greater joy in every social interaction. By nurturing only the most meaningful relationships, he ended up with fewer social contacts overall, but the quality of his social life increased dramatically.

When you retire, you'll likely say goodbye to many important relationships—clients and perhaps even colleagues who no longer share your daily world. To help ease the transition and counter the sense of loss, make it a priority to strengthen your social connections in new and meaningful ways. Doing so can help you navigate this major life change with greater ease and fulfillment.

Get started on connecting with these important relationships now, and you will be highly rewarded for the effort when you retire.

—Exercise—

Enhancing Your Social Connections

This exercise will help you to understand your social connections that need to be enhanced and improved in retirement. In the left column, make a list of the people you genuinely desire to spend more time with. Then, in the right column, think of an idea or two of how you might connect.

Person You Value	How You Can Develop a Connection
My sister	Ask her to brunch on Sundays

Your Retirement Identity

The closer you get to retirement, the more important it is to plan your life activities. In a webinar for the Center for the Study of Aging and Clinical Applications, Freire and Margolies (2024) reviewed several distinct orientations that they considered retirement identities. You may immediately recognize one or more of these in yourself as you think about how you will structure your retirement:

- **Task doers:** These individuals envision continuing to work in some capacity well past their retirement age, or they retire from their place of employment only to continue to be engaged in work of some type. These would include people who volunteer, whether using their already honed skills from their job or helping in a community program, such as tutoring children or helping seniors with annual taxes. (No, you don't have to be an accountant for this one.)
- **Leisure seekers:** These are the people who have been waiting for retirement to focus on recreation. They might be waiting for enough time to go fishing or canoeing as often as possible, to improve their pickleball game, or to play duplicate bridge for the first time. They may be eager to get to their vacation getaway on a lake or in the mountains and spend time just enjoying it.
- **Searching for calm:** This would be the category of people who want to focus on spiritual life and meditation. Searching for calm can describe those who want to rest, to have a life with limited obligations and lots of time to relax in whatever way makes them feel best. They may want to pursue hobbies, but whatever they choose, it will be time without demands.
- **Explorers:** Some people are eager for retirement so they can take off: traveling the world, seeing every National Park, attending culinary school (finally!), practicing carpentry, or taking action in other ways so they can learn new things. They may not even know all the ways they want to explore, but they will stay open to adventure.
- **Family extenders:** For some approaching retirement, time with family is their primary goal. They may have had a spouse who is retired and waiting to do things together, or they may have longed for extended time with grandchildren. Their meaningful relationships will give them great satisfaction.
- **Out of focus:** We hope that you will not fall into this category of people like Joanna, who took nearly seven years to settle into her identity as a gardener,

eventually growing food and creating beauty to give her a sense of meaning. Most therapists in this category are likely those who were forced into retirement and did not have the opportunity to plan what their time would look like. The time of unfocused activity typically creates dissatisfaction with retired life. But if you find yourself in this category, you can use the activities in this chapter to gain sharper focus on your personal satisfaction.

You can also gain insight about what you might want to do in retirement based on choices you have made already. LaDonna, a licensed professional counselor, had always had an interest in art, and in fact, she had an undergraduate degree in art history. She thought she might want to teach, but she knew she did not want to go through all of the complications of getting certified to teach, nor did she want to be tied down if she did not like it. She contacted her local art museum and found that its docent program allowed her to use her knowledge and interest to work as a guide in the museum—for her, a perfect combination of making her knowledge useful without the commitments of preparing classes and grading papers.

Henry, a psychologist, wanted to travel more. He took an extended trip to Nepal the year before he retired and found an emotional connection there he had never anticipated. Now that he has retired, he is involved in groups that support Nepalese children, and he plans to travel there each year to deepen his sense of belonging and commitment.

Your ability to plan and advance new experiences before you retire can open doors later for retirement activities and goals.

Finding Balance in Retirement

Expect that your plans for how to *be* in retirement will alter as you find the balance between your various needs. Successful balance can start with assessing yourself as you are now, outside of your work.

Geoffrey was just giving up his clinical practice in a rural area when he turned seventy-five. He and his wife were in good health but realized living out in the country might become a problem if driving got harder or if one of them developed health issues. They lived a long way from good medical care. They opted to move to an independent living setting that would allow progressive levels of care. In the new setting, Geoffrey realized that his wife was happy to have so many people with whom to socialize, but he was miserable. He had not considered the communal nature of what was basically apartment living. After being in the country on acres of land, Geoffrey needed to work out how to get enough privacy and quiet time. He began to collect his notes and journals and think about writing a book. He said, "There is nothing like writing to give you all the time you need to be quiet. And no one wants to hear you talk about it!" He laughed his trademark mischievous chuckle and declared, "Now I just have to convince my wife to take some of our meals alone with me in our apartment, at least some of the time!"

When I (Margaret) formally retired from clinical work, I threw myself into activities. I quickly got lost in *doing*, and, when I was finding it hard to keep track of days, it was partly because I was operating on other people's schedules, saying yes to everything that was asked of me by others. I had time! I would do it!

I had to step back and ask myself, yet again, what activities were making me feel delighted and happy while also making me feel meaningful and useful in the world. I resigned from one volunteer job I committed to, a very unusual action for me, because I began to resent the demands that were making my life too hectic. That was *not* what I had in mind for a happy retirement. I had not planned well enough ahead of retiring and had to make adjustments as I went. Striking the balance between being useful and being far too busy took a bit of time to get right.

Your favorite activities and interests can help you think about your identity and also formulate a plan for successful balance in retirement:

- **Hobbies:** A host of activities qualify as hobbies, so don't limit your assessment too narrowly. A hobby could be any activity that interests you, that you devote time to regularly, and that offers mental as well as physical stimulation. For example, you may spend time watching your grandchild several days a week; that may make you feel very useful, but is it an activity that stimulates your mind or body? Think of how different that is from improving your carpentry skills, practicing a musical instrument, creating art, writing, doing needlework, or gardening. Those activities involve some measure of study and even daily focus. One of our colleagues found an organization that assigns her to independent living and nursing facilities to play the piano and lead sing-alongs. She can do this as many days a week as she cares to, but when she wants a break or travels, there is no weekly commitment.
- **Keeping yourself healthy:** Aside from eating habits, find ways to move your body every day. You can practice yoga, dance, run marathons, stretch, lift weights, do

water aerobics, ride bicycles, hike, ski, or do other kinds of physical exercise. One of our colleagues decided to take ballet for seniors, having always wanted to dance!

- **Travel:** The extra time retirement offers will allow for more extended trips if this is your desire. Be sure to take into consideration your current level of vigor and physical ability before planning to travel or vacation. You might go on a road trip, cruise the ocean, go outdoors, or visit a city for its museums and restaurants.
- **Friendships:** It takes time to develop friendships fully, yet retirement offers the opportunity to start friendships based on criteria other than shared work experiences. Approaching retirement, review relationships with colleagues and acquaintances outside of your work, and begin to nurture those more deliberately. It will ease your shift into retirement to have friends you can share time with.
- **Community caring:** Feeling connected is vital to a healthy retirement. One particularly powerful way to find meaning and feel useful and connected is to participate in community organizations that do work you admire. You can explore these before retirement so you can choose wisely where to devote your newfound time when you stop working. You might be a member of a board, mentor with programs like Big Brothers and Big Sisters, participate in charities, or create scholarships within the community.
- **Causes:** Many older adults express their desire to be activists for causes that are meaningful to them, and some report becoming politically active or devoting time to causes for which they are passionate, such as animal welfare, the environment, hospice care, or humanitarian causes. As you envision your activities in retirement, do you see yourself participating in personal causes? Perhaps you see yourself working on policy or fundraising at local, national, or international levels?
- **Spiritual exploration:** Many people we surveyed commented on appreciating retirement as an opportunity to deepen their spiritual practices. Some wanted time to meditate, and others wanted to participate in their religious organizations. They indicated that time to "be" was part of the benefit of working less. Do you see yourself wanting time to read and reflect or to be quiet and think? You may want to explore ahead of retirement via a retreat or a course of study to deepen your awareness of options to enrich your inner life.

—Exercise—

Your Identity in Retirement

This exercise will help you to figure out your identity in retirement. Whether you are looking forward to complete relaxation or days packed with activities, planning for how you will spend your days will provide you with more connection, meaning, and purpose.

Hobbies: What would you like to do in your spare time? How do these activities stimulate your mind or body? Is there anything you would like to learn to do?

____

____

____

____

Health: How do you keep yourself healthy? Do you see yourself in retirement doing more of those activities? Are there any new activities you'd like to try?

____

____

____

____

Travel: What kind of travel are you currently able to do and what do you enjoy? Do you currently have a partner or close friend or a group with whom you travel? How do you choose where and what kind of trip you would take?

____

____

____

____

Friendship: What friendships do you currently have? Are there friends with whom you want to spend more time? What activities would you like to do with your friends?

____

____

____

____

Community: Are you currently active in community organizations? Are there ways you anticipate doing more (or perhaps less) when you retire? Is there a part of the community you'd like to begin working with?

____

____

____

____

Causes: Are you passionate about any causes? What are you already doing, and what do you want to do more of?

____

____

____

____

Spiritual exploration: Are you interested in time for reflection or quiet or study? Is there a particular person, group, or place you want to pursue to expand your current practice?

____

____

____

____

Moving Forward

Being creative about your plan for retirement might be easy for you—or not. The exercises in this chapter intend to focus your attention on how your life values can play into retirement choices, helping you maintain a coherent identity, and facilitate the stage of development that Erikson calls *integrity*.

The next chapter will help you envision how that life might look, completing the generativity stage and moving toward integrity and satisfaction. In chapter 12, we invite you to meet your future self and preview what a day in your retirement can feel like.

—Chapter 12—

Meeting Your Future Self

Your sense of time changes in retirement. Laurel called her friend, who had organized a meeting she planned to attend, to apologize. "I am so sorry. I missed meeting you today for lunch." She explained, "All day I thought it was Monday and we were going to meet tomorrow. But when I heard the news talking about today as *Tuesday,* I realized with a jolt that I had missed a day because yesterday was a holiday. I just can't get used to not having an automatic calendar in my head set by when I work!"

Therapists live by the clock, watching as clients rotate in and out of sessions hour after hour. But Laurel, early in her retirement, is no longer "clocking in," following regular work hours, or even keeping a regular weekly pattern.

"This is getting embarrassing," she said. "I find myself all settled in, ready to turn on a program or open a book, and I get a text wondering why I am not at the meeting. Even worse, I missed the FaceTime call I had promised to my little granddaughter. I just forgot. It was not linked to anything, the way it always was in the days before I retired."

Once you retire, time is not linked to the passing hour of a session. If you worked at an agency or organization, the flow of meetings would have been marked by the punctuation of weekends. If your work revolved around the academic calendar or the season of the year when grant writing is at a fever pitch, you would have had a more seasonal element to show time passing.

If your work shapes your experience of time, work and time can become bound together. When you retire, time must find a new orientation. Managing time is just one aspect of retirement that can be difficult to control until you're actually in that phase of life. How you use your time in retirement is an important consideration when predicting what your "new normal" will look like. In retirement, what was once considered unusual or temporary has now become the expected state of affairs.

The New Normal: Time and Friends

In earlier chapters, you identified your push factors: the reasons you need to leave your career. These are powerful retirement motivators. You then noted your pull factors: the positives that draw you toward retirement. This process is central to understanding when to retire. While push factors might be the most powerful reasons for *needing* to retire, pull factors make it clear why you *want* to retire. Knowing what pushes and pulls you provides the encouragement to walk away from work you love and move toward the future, pursuing the activities you desire. It helps clarify your timing to shift into action. In this workbook, you have also explored both your professional and personal identity, examined how to end therapy well with those who depend on you, and then took steps to get prepared with a plan and logistics.

Now what? Are you ready to spring into action? In the action stage, you rely on sensing when and how to take the next steps into retirement. But no matter how well prepared you may feel, some things about retirement may take you by surprise. The need to manage time differently is one of them.

When I (Lynn) got trained in neurolinguistic programming early in my career, my trainer John Grinder used to make a distinction about time. He said that some people were "in time"—meaning that they stored time internally and showed up when the time felt right, often late for appointments, instead of watching the clock. Others (like me), were consistently "on time" and inveterate clock watchers, invariably prompt. Carl Jung (1972) believed that time was relative—if we could let go of linear perception, we could see the synchronicity between past, present, and future.

In retirement, your relationship to time may run on a different current. How do you keep yourself oriented to passing days, remember your plans and complete them, or stay as busy or productive as you desire when time seems to move at a different pace?

I (Margaret) had expertly juggled a variety of activities during my career. I had absolutely *loved* how my work life was not the same old same old every day. I had different clients each day, I had different meetings, and I traveled somewhere to teach seminars several times a month. I had a schedule, often a tight one, to get everything done, and I consulted it often. Then, I retired. I thought I did not need to look at a schedule, and found myself, like Laurel, missing things I had agreed to show up for even though I had written it down—somewhere. In retirement, I was shocked at my new time-challenged self, previously having been so aware of what I had to do on a specific day.

As I tearfully apologized on a Saturday morning to my dear friend Lurlene for forgetting our long-planned phone call the previous Thursday night, I explained that I was cranky and not feeling myself at all. Lurlene said to me in her wisest tone of voice and charming Southern accent, "Darlin', get yourself a big paper calendar, a month-at-a-glance preferably. And put it somewhere that it will be the first thing you see every day. You have got yourself all detached from the passage of days. I suggest you put it next to your coffee pot. If you do that, you won't have to keep apologizing to everyone."

She intuited my need; without a schedule that no longer looked or felt familiar, I needed to have a tangible, spatial view of how the new day fit into a week. I followed her advice, and every day for at least a year, I looked at that calendar, on which I had everything from important daily activities to birthdays to remember. I gradually stopped losing track of days.

The meaning of my story goes beyond the importance of the calendar or even my need to adjust to a new sense of time. It emphasizes how crucial it is to have the support of someone who knows you well enough to help you identify your stumbling blocks. A key part of the new normal in retirement is knowing who will be there for you.

In retirement, who can you rely on to be honest when your mood shifts? Who can problem-solve with you—or for you? Who can point out your mistakes without getting angry and still appreciate all you have to offer and everything your retirement allows?

Use your retirement journal to reflect more on the new normal of retirement.

RETIREMENT JOURNAL

The New Normal

Reflect on the following prompts in your retirement journal to help you think about the new normal of retirement in terms of time and relationships:

New Normal Time

- What kind of time do I want to adopt in retirement: being "in" time or being "on" time?
    - If "in" time, how will I plan to keep track of my days and my schedule?
    - If "on" time, how will I allow myself to stop and smell the roses?
- What new regular activities, such as exercise class or grandchild care, will I do and on what days?
- What will I make space for so that I don't feel rushed or pressured?
- What activities that I have been doing, such as exercise, board meetings, or rotary club, will remain on my schedule? Will they occur at the same times and days as before?
- If my retirement involves moving to a new area or spending extended time away from home, (e.g., a few months away in a vacation home), which activities will be part of my weekly plan when I am there? What time can I allow with no agenda?
- What does rest and relaxation mean to me in terms of spending time?

New Normal Friends

- Who among my family and friends can I count on for honest support?
- How will I tell them what I might need?
- How will we be sure to check in with each other about how I am doing with retirement? (e.g., invite them to pay attention and share their observations for at least the first six months of retirement via a regular coffee date or phone call that specifically includes feedback)
- Who would be wonderful to have in my circle when I retire? How do I bring them in if they are not already there?
- How will I share my goals with others? (If you identified any specific goals in your work on pull factors, identify the friends or family who are most able to specifically support the items in the following list.)
    - Passions
    - Creative goals
    - Physical goals
    - Family goals
    - Health goals

Your New Status

Another surprise waiting to happen is the simple act of claiming a new status: that of being retired. For example, if you are asked what you do and you say, "I am retired," how will that feel to you? How do you imagine others might respond? In the early stages of retirement, you may get disconcerted by stating this new standing as well as noticing your own reactions to others' comments on your retirement.

The response you get will depend on who you're speaking with and their views on work, retirement, and aging. Each conversation may lead to a different interaction, shaped by how you frame your retirement and how others relate to it. Plan to notice what people say when you claim your new status and then watch how you feel about what they say. You may hear responses like these:

- **"What did you do before?"** This shifts you back to defining your work life. What level of interest do others show about what you previously did? How eagerly do you leap into a description of your prior job?
- **"Oh."** No interest shown. Where do you take the conversation? Are you feeling devalued and worthless without work, or do you launch into a description of how glad you are to have the time for your new activities?
- **"So what are you doing now that you are a person of leisure?"** Are you ready to be enthused about your new life? Do you feel defensive that you are not working even though the other person does not specifically indicate you should be? Do you feel obliged to represent yourself in some way that "puffs you up" but does not feel entirely genuine? Do you feel embarrassed about what you are doing with your time?
- **"Congratulations!"** How do you personally take this? Are you appreciative, resentful, puzzled, irritated, or worthy? It depends on how well you know the person saying this and whether they know any of the details of your retirement decision.

Regardless of others' intent, so many of your own subtle attitudes about retirement will be revealed by your reactions. For example, does it feel weird, as if you are being congratulated on having given up the most important thing in your life? Or are you taken aback, as if the person is being insensitive, congratulating you on a decision you were forced to make? Does it feel absurd, as if you are being congratulated for getting old? Or do you appreciate this as sincere, for doing so well in your career that you can now enjoy different aspects of life?

When you announce your retirement, people's reactions can vary widely depending on their relationship with you, their own perspective on retirement, and the context in which the announcement is made. Use your retirement journal to imagine how you may feel when you announce your new status.

RETIREMENT JOURNAL

Announcing Your Retirement

Here are some common things people might say. Imagine the different tones and emotions these comments could convey. Write down your potential emotional reactions, feelings, or any answers you would give to those people who are:

- Curious about your career
- Uninterested in you if you are not employed
- Curious about how you spend your time
- Congratulatory

A New Introduction

Another new normal skill you may need post-retirement, regardless of the various situations you find yourself in, is having an introduction. How do you want to talk about who you are?

What will you lead with if not your job title? It can feel awkward introducing yourself when you don't have a work-related hook. A little planning ahead can make these situations easier, especially if you're not naturally outgoing. Some things, like your hobbies or activities, are simple to bring up in conversation. For instance, mentioning that you're enjoying your newfound time to play golf, join a book club, plant a garden, go fly fishing, or participate in community theater isn't particularly revealing, but it provides a natural way to share who you are. You can tailor how you present these interests depending on the situation.

If you're more reticent or haven't had to introduce yourself socially in this way before, it can be helpful to plan ahead. Think about how you'll share your passions with others so you feel more comfortable when the moment arises.

—*Exercise*—

A New Introduction

Write out how you might introduce yourself in retirement for each of the different scenarios provided here.

You are attending a meeting for an organization you want to volunteer in. You have the same interests as others in the group—because they are also there to volunteer. When asked to tell the group something about yourself, what will you say?

____

____

You are at a social event, like a block party or a gathering at a friend's house. Your friend introduces you to someone new. What do you want to say when asked, "What do you do?"

____

____

What is the most creative new introduction you could offer?

____

____

What is a playful way to establish yourself as retired?

____

____

What is an introduction that best suits your personality and authenticity?

____

____

Feeling Invisible in Retirement

One thing that women of retirement age remark on is feeling invisible. It is not just that they are no longer looked at or pursued for romantic reasons as they were when they were younger—it is that they may no longer be seen at all. They are overlooked or not seen as capable, worthy, or valuable. This has become a social phenomenon called the *Invisible Woman Syndrome*. In the TV series *Matlock* (2024), Kathy Bates stars as a seventy-plus-year-old woman—a stellar attorney still capable of "swimming with the sharks" in legal battles. The fact that she gets unnoticed due to her age creates a serious challenge, but at times, it offers her an advantage. She can gather information without being seen. Being invisible, for anyone who is aging, has its pros and cons.

I (Margaret) have noted that when I was younger and single and traveling for work constantly, the chances were high that if I sat next to a man on a flight, he would start a conversation. More than one of those conversations ended with making a plan to meet after we got off our flight. Now in my seventies, still single, the only time a man talks to me on a plane is to ask me if I need help wrestling my bag into an overhead bin. I always say yes, of course, because I believe in helping people feel good about themselves! But if I weren't hoisting a bag, as long as I behave appropriately, no one would notice I am on the flight.

Although we change physically, we still see ourselves as we know ourselves to be—capable, useful, and valuable individuals. If we are not defined by our careers, people may judge us based primarily on our appearance. Time has faded the cover of our book, at least for most of us. We are grayer, our faces are lined, and, typically, we may not appear as vigorous as we feel, even if we are not impaired.

Therapists have a special relationship with invisibility. In our work, we are not the center of attention. We let our clients be at the fore. Their needs and ideas and wishes are primary. We listen and mask our immediate reactions, needs, and opinions. For some, this means that we become accustomed to inhabiting the (necessary) background position of the therapist. But when stepping out of the therapy setting into retirement, we may find that we are invisible in groups where we could have more presence.

An additional factor in feeling invisible relates to personality, specifically the inclination toward introversion—something common among many therapists. Jung (1923) described introversion as an energetic preference: Some people are energized by being around others, while others are restored by solitude. Being introverted doesn't mean not being sociable when in groups or disliking people. Rather, an introverted person might feel drained after spending time in large groups and long for quiet moments alone to recharge. Introverts also tend to value time to reflect and process information before speaking, allowing for deeper integration of ideas. This temperament is well-suited to the work of a therapist.

I (Lynn) am an introvert. At a recent two-hour dinner party with old friends, I realized I hadn't spoken once. I listened, smiled, and stayed engaged, but I didn't feel the need to contribute verbally. Part of this may have been a carryover from a long day of work in my role as a therapist, where I naturally remain quiet. Or perhaps I was simply tired, as talking can drain energy for an introvert. But I think it's more than that. I'm comfortable with silence, as many therapists are. I can easily take a backseat in group conversations. Socializing, however, requires me to set aside that internalization, step forward, and participate. I can imagine that in retirement, much of my time will be social, and when meeting new people, I'll need to do more than just observe from the sidelines. I'll have to actively connect rather than just smile and listen.

As you head into retirement, you might find yourself slipping into the background, much like wearing Harry Potter's invisibility cloak. Harry saw and heard everything going on, but others did not see him. Silence and listening can create a similar effect—you're aware of everything happening around you, but others may not notice you unless you speak. In this metaphor, the question becomes: Are you ready to speak up more in social settings and step into a greater presence as you retire?

Self-Presentation in Retirement

When meeting new people and introducing ourselves, we often highlight what we want them to see. As we grow older, we tend to focus on our strengths, shaping how others perceive us. We become accustomed to describing ourselves, effectively telling people what they should notice. But in retirement, we have the opportunity to rethink that self-description. The question becomes: How do you want to appear in the eyes of others?

Are there things you want people to know about you, or perhaps qualities you hope they'll observe in your character without you needing to say a word? These are not necessarily things you announce. By living out your values in everyday interactions, others will come to understand who you are—but that takes time. However, you can immediately influence what people notice and how they perceive you through the way you present yourself.

For women, retirement often brings decisions about how much time to spend on personal appearance once the daily demands of working are reduced. People do make judgments about who you are based on your clothing and overall appearance. Just observe people in a grocery store. What assumptions do you make about them? We all do it: Is the smartly dressed woman a business executive just picking up a few things for dinner? Will she have to eat alone, or is someone waiting for her? Is the man in sweats, a baseball cap, and a scruffy beard having a slow day, stocking up to watch football with friends, or is he depressed? Is the woman in athletic wear heading home from a workout at the gym, or is she dashing about on a hectic day before the kids get out of school? It's natural to make these assumptions. Think about your own biases.

Others also make assumptions about you when you're out in public. Many psychotherapists retiring are not leaving their communities; instead, they're starting new roles as volunteers or joining clubs and organizations they've long wanted to be part of. As you engage in new activities or social roles, those same factors—how you present yourself—play a role in how you're seen.

Retirement gives you new freedom to show up the way you want. Are you someone who has been biding her time until she can stop putting on makeup every day and who is happy to wear casual clothes? Does retirement give you a chance to be more playful and creative with a different style, one that would not have worked in the office? Alternately, does the idea of having no reason to dress more formally depress you? Do you want a reason to continue taking time with your appearance every day, or do you enjoy the freedom of not doing your hair and makeup as when you went into work? You can make those choices based on who you will see and what impression you want to make.

Danielle, an interviewee, shared her delight in donating all her business attire to a local "Dress for Success" charity, which helps women find outfits for job interviews. She explained that if she has to dress for a Zoom meeting, she's likely to throw on a nice sweater over her yoga clothes, assuming that others will understand the outfit isn't the focus of the meeting.

However, she also knows how to adapt for different situations. "When I needed to meet a new primary care physician, I made sure to do it all—hair, makeup, and good clothes—because I wanted that young doctor to see a capable, attractive, and competent woman, not just an older person. I want him to see someone who can understand everything he says. And I'm going to make sure he knows I have a PhD before he starts talking down to me."

Danielle's approach is a reminder of how our appearance sends a message before any words are exchanged. She is realistic about how people form impressions based on what they see, and she is aware that she can shape that perception.

RETIREMENT JOURNAL

Presenting Yourself

Think about or anticipate your ideas of self-presentation when you retire by answering the following prompts in your retirement journal:

- How do I want to appear?
- Will different environments influence how I present myself?
- What shift in my current appearance would signal the following:
    - Independent
    - Brave
    - Competent
    - Intriguing
    - Joyful
    - Comfortable
    - Alluring
    - Other

Focusing on the Present

Anne, retired for a year after a career as a full-time clinician, has recently become acquainted with a fairly large number of retired women at a social club. She observes how women introduce themselves to each other. Some live in the past and talk about what used to be. Others live in the future with a focus on the next bright shiny object: a trip, a project, or an upcoming family event. The women Anne likes best are the ones who, like her, try to live in the present.

She asks questions to promote conversation about the women's present-day activities: What books are you reading? Where do you like to walk? What brings a smile to your face now?

"These are questions about who we are today," she said. "Even in my stories about my past, I try to find ways of describing what I did in the context of who I am today." To jumpstart your new normal, find ways to talk about the present person you are in retirement.

—Exercise—

Present-Day You

Define a present-oriented way to share about yourself and your life.

What are three things you want people to know about you in the first hour you spend with them?

____

____

____

How do your daily activities reflect your values?

____

____

____

What are you most interested in today?

____

____

____

How did your career inform who you are now?

____

____

____

What do you think is best about this next stage of life?

____

____

____

Imagining Your Future

Can you imagine your future in retirement? In our workshops, we offer a guided imagery exercise, which we will provide later in this chapter. It allows you to spend a day in your future, once you are fully retired, helping you to visualize and feel what retirement might bring.

Many therapists are familiar with the benefits of guided imagery. The very act of imagining—using your senses to create an experience shaped by emotions, thoughts, and desires—can influence your creativity, behavior, and self-discovery. Therapists who use imagery as a healing tool believe that imagining future scenarios can subtly shift outcomes.

For instance, envisioning yourself as healthy and vigorous can motivate both your brain and body to take action. Imagining yourself at the gym, working out with satisfaction, may make you more likely to go, even on days when gloomy weather tempts you to stay home with another cup of coffee.

You may have used guided imagery with clients in your practice. Neurobiological research on trauma shows that we can become the embodiment of our own imagination. Simply recalling emotional pain can activate the brain in the same way it did when the trauma originally occurred, releasing similar neurochemicals. Psychotherapists help clients stop rehearsing guilt, fear, regret, and other negative emotions tied to past experiences. Instead, we guide them toward calm and acceptance, interrupting the brain's activation of pain so that memories no longer trigger emotional distress. As a therapist, you may guide clients in this way, even if you didn't realize you were actively changing their brain.

This applies identically to experiencing past emotions of joy and delight. Your brain recreates the rewards of those events, and you can again feel the positive emotions. It is why we love to look at pictures of vacations, weddings, graduations, parties, and our children throughout the years. The act of remembering brings up all the rewarding feelings—because the brain is releasing all the neurochemicals that light up the reward network in the brain. This is why merely *thinking* of seeing your partner or your best friend, eating chocolate cake, swimming in the ocean, or snuggling in bed on a cold morning makes you feel good. Your brain gives you a little fizz of pleasure.

The same brain activity is relevant to envisioning your future in retirement. When you imagine how you will be in the future, your brain takes note. You are preparing your brain to observe and be fully ready to react to the new experiences. For example, when you anticipate the pleasure of being outside for a walk, your brain is releasing chemicals and alerting your reward network, the same way it will when you actually take your walk. This is like pre-fun. It is already rewarding, even if at a lesser level of intensity than when you actually go for that walk.

Now that you've had that pre-fun because your brain lit up the reward network, when you do take that walk, you will be quicker to notice what you like about it, and your brain will be primed to react to the pleasure. The walk will be more fun than it would be with no positive anticipation. With preparation of anticipation, your brain is ready to release the chemicals of reward and it begins that process more quickly.

There is an even more significant aspect of imaging your future. As you visualize how you want things to be, you can start moving yourself to make it happen. By previewing your possible future, you can be more intentional about those choices because of your clarity of what you want. You are shaping your future whenever you imagine how you want it to be, even if you do this without awareness and intention.

The power of imagining changes your brain and affects your perceptions and reactions. It also influences how your physical body will respond to what you imagine. Bernie Siegel (1999) and Belleruth Naparstek (1995) are two well-known practitioners who, among other topics, write about how imagery changes the physical body. They describe this in relation to recovery from illness or surgery and to other health challenges. They posit that we can bring into reality that which we imagine for ourselves. The experience of imagery can provide us with new information, allowing us to redefine our goals both at a conscious, intentional level and at a more unconscious level, influencing the ways we create our future.

The old adage "Be careful what you wish for" highlights a potential downside to the process when it's not fully understood. For example, you might wish for things without considering their full implications. You could feel burned out and exhausted, and in your guided imagery, wish in retirement to be left alone without anyone bothering you. However, once you're feeling more resilient, you may find that you crave more human connection to feel whole.

Another downside is wishing without a plan of action. This can turn the process into a passive exercise—one that leaves you without any strategy to make a change. Without accompanying movement or proactive steps, wishing on its own may leave you feeling deprived, sad, or even depressed.

On the flip side, when you visualize having a goal, you see yourself in action, in the service of that goal. This helps you feel that you're already on your way to achieving it. This is what we hope will happen as you visualize your retirement. By imagining your future proactively, you not only give yourself the power to envision how things might unfold, but you also gain new insights that help redefine your goals and take steps toward them. Visualization allows you to self-correct as well, by previewing what you thought you wanted but didn't fully explore. Then you can tweak your wants and wishes to reflect your reality.

Joseph, a workshop participant, found that the guided imagery exercise helped clarify what his retirement might feel like based on his current thoughts and desires. "I see what's coming, and it's not exactly what I want," he said. "Unless I make some changes, my retired life will look like my weekends—just every day will be a weekend day." When asked how that would feel, he replied, "I love my weekends, but I don't want to lose the specialness of having a day off. I need to figure out how to keep the things I enjoy about my weekends without losing their distinctiveness."

The guided imagery exercise gave him a prediction of his potential future and the opportunity to improve it, ensuring that retirement could be what he truly needs and wants.

The following exercise is a visualization to help you see yourself as a retired person. As you reflect on the image, try to imagine this future experience as vividly as possible. Focus on the details in the imagery using all five senses—the smells, sounds, tastes, sights, and touch. Not everyone can imagine every sense, so simply accept the ones that occur in your experience.

—*Exercise*—

Meeting Your Future Self

It can be easier to experience this visualization if you ask someone to read this to you, or you can record yourself and then listen back; in doing so, you can really immerse yourself in the experience. Each step and prompt needs to be followed with sufficient silence to give you time to process—this can be seconds or minutes. If someone else is reading this to you, give them feedback on whether you need more or less time between prompts. After you have completed the guided imagery, take time to write about your experience.

Close your eyes, be relaxed, and imagine a time in the future, as clearly as you can. Your retirement date has arrived! You took the next step. You left your office or place of work and have been fully retired for a month. Today is a typical retirement day for you, one that you may have anticipated or one that has some surprises for you. Allow your internal senses—what you can see, hear, feel, smell, taste, and be aware of—to inform your experience as you notice:

- You have just woken up; it is morning. Where are you living?
- What time do you arise?
- What are the first things you do when you get out of bed?
- Do you start the day with a stretch, feeling muscles relax and energize?
- Perhaps you drink a cup of coffee or tea? Smell the brew and feel the cup in your hand.
- What is the weather like outside? What does the air smell like? What does the sky look like? Are you outside, or watching it through an open window?
- What activities will occupy your day?
- Are you going out in nature, or staying in to enjoy your free time to draw, write, needlepoint, read the paper, or watch a favorite program?

- What are you wearing? Will you wear specific clothes for the activities you have planned? How do these clothes feel on your body?
- How do you feel physically? What is your energy like on this day?
- Who will be around you on this day, and when and how will you spend time with those people?
- What are you eating? You have all the time you need to enjoy your meals. Are you taking pleasure in eating healthily or cooking? Who shares meals with you?
- What else does the day include? Allow the fullness of the day to unfold.
- How do you end your day? Are you alone or with someone? Does it end quietly? Do you see yourself reading, watching TV, having a glass of wine or a cup of tea with your partner, or lying in bed?
- As you reflect back on the day, how do you feel? What was best about it? What brought you satisfaction and appreciation?
- What do you look forward to doing tomorrow?

Now write what you have visualized; do this quickly, but with as much detail as possible.

When you complete the writing, how do you feel? What did you learn? What will you remember from this imagery?

When we offer the exercise *Meeting Your Future Self* in our workshops and webinars, participants often have striking and dramatic reactions. Many experience moments of revelation in which they gain a vivid sense of what it feels like to be retired. These moments can evoke a wide range of emotions, and people are often surprised by what emerges—things they hadn't anticipated. In these moments, the future becomes more tangible and possible.

Participants in our workshops experience this guided imagery exercise in a variety of ways:

- Angela had been feeling anxious about what retirement would be like, wondering if she could ever imagine being content without the daily organization of work. Yet, when she imagined the scene of morning coffee on her porch and having time to go to a yoga class to start her day—rather than hustling to begin a long commute—she felt a deep sense of longing. She wanted a peaceful start to each day. "I didn't realize that I might *not* be bored in retirement, and that I might, in fact, find joy in having time to drink coffee, do morning yoga, or meet a friend for lunch without a time deadline. I miss out on so much."
- Correen had a somewhat different reaction; her future self was energized. "I can hardly wait to get at this now," she enthused. "I could see myself at meetings organizing with people against gun violence. I visualized handing out gun safety information at summer street fairs and going to the state legislature to advocate for passage of new laws. I feel passionate about this cause because my neighborhood school had an active shooter incident—thank God no one died, but change is going to be up to us older folks with time to be activists."
- Elizabeth commented that her anxiety level dropped after the exercise. She did not see herself as ever being able to retire completely until she absolutely cannot work, needing to supplement her meager retirement income with continued work. She used the visualization to imagine a life in which she gives herself permission to plan on working only two days a week and filling the rest of her week with self-care, such as more exercise, more sleep, and more time with her grandchildren who live nearby. "I always think I don't have time, but imagining a genuine semiretirement, putting boundaries on when I work and preserving time for myself, felt doable for the first time. This could happen!"
- In our workshops, Margaret guides participants through this exercise, so I (Lynn) have also had the pleasure of getting to listen to her instructions with closed

eyes, meeting my future self, and experiencing a day in retirement. I am not yet retired and may not be for several years, so this chance to preview my future is important for me. I notice that time slows down in this potential future. Much is the same as it is now, but what is different is that I am very relaxed in my body. I see myself walking on a path near the park next to my current home, but my walk is not hurried (as it often is when I am trying to get my steps in before my next task.) Instead, I feel like I have all the time in the world and can see and hear nature without needing to look away. I feel a sense of openness and rest. In the imaginal space, I go through the day, an ordinary day, with nothing special planned. But I feel quiet, at ease, and content. I know that there are things to do during this day, but they feel like they are mostly the things I want to do, not things I have to do.

Moving Forward

Do you feel alone in your process of retirement? Many therapists tell us that their isolation during the various stages of retiring makes for a solitary journey. In the coda, which follows this chapter, we encourage you to shift perspective and remember that even if you don't know anyone who is retiring in the same time or manner that you are, chances are you are part of a larger community. Eventually, every one of us will join this group, and we will all face the same emotions and challenges you may be encountering.

So as you advance to the coda, welcome to the neighborhood! You will read direct comments and reflections from others to see how they have navigated or are currently navigating their retirement. If you struggle with a sense of isolation, the coda can help you to feel connected to the larger conversation of retirement.

Coda: Other Voices, Other Rooms

Retirement can be a lonely time for therapists, with few opportunities to share experiences with colleagues who are navigating it themselves. Despite being part of a deeply relational profession, many therapists find themselves isolated during this transition. There are countless resources about starting and sustaining a therapy practice, yet very few address how to bring one to a thoughtful close. It's no surprise that those nearing retirement often feel alone.

Before writing on this topic, we searched for retirement resources tailored to our profession—and were struck by how little exists. There are few articles, books, courses, or even general guidance to help therapists consider how, when, and why to retire. Ending a practice is rarely, if ever, addressed in graduate or postgraduate programs, and most supervision or training groups do not include it in their scope.

One exception we found was Lynn's professional social work association, the Greater Washington Society for Clinical Social Work (gwscsw.org), which sponsors peer support groups for those who have retired or are preparing to retire. With nearly ten active groups in the Washington, DC area, we gathered valuable insights from members willing to share their experiences.

However, as we expanded our reach nationally through workshops and presentations, we discovered that these retirement support groups are rare. If you don't know any colleagues retiring in a similar way or timeframe, you may feel as though you're walking this path solo. It's not uncommon for therapists to face retirement without meaningful support or connection.

Over the past five years, as we've studied, taught, and written about this topic, we've had the privilege of hearing from many therapists about their retirement journeys. Now, in this final section of the book, we offer you the chance to hear from them too.

Here, we invite you to connect with the voices of colleagues in one of the four stages of the Readiness for Retirement Model: precontemplation, contemplation, preparation, and action. These reflections come from real conversations and responses gathered throughout our research. Some are compilations, drawn from similar remarks made by multiple therapists. All comments are used with permission, and identifying details—such as names, licensure, and practice locations—have been removed to preserve confidentiality. In some cases, the quotes have been lightly edited for readability or shortened to highlight key points.

As you read, we hope these voices will validate your own thoughts and feelings, or offer new insights as you navigate this transition. Retirement is still a relatively new topic in our field, and we are all learning together—about its practical challenges, emotional layers, and deep personal meaning.

Listen as others reflect on their experience at each stage of readiness, beginning with precontemplation. After each section, we invite you to add your voice through the exercise that follows.

Precontemplation: "Once you find your calling to be a therapist, why would you ever leave?"

Those struggling with *Precontemplation: The Stay or Go Dilemma* (chapters 1–3) tell us that they are thinking about the need for change, but not in a planful or serious way. This awareness may feel secretive or tinged with denial as they avoid discussing the issue and hesitate to openly acknowledge to others, even close friends or family, that retirement is approaching. Therapists at this stage mention competing agendas: the compelling nature of their work versus anxiety around change. There is a pull to maintain the same work pace and level of engagement, yet also a sense of internal conflict. This ambivalence is a defining feature of the precontemplation stage.

As you read what others say, note the ties that we all have to our professional identity that need to be loosened, even slightly, to help advance us into more readiness.

> I love being a therapist. I love the analysis of people and personal reflection inherent in the work, but also the feeling of doing something meaningful. I discovered I could help people suffering from panic and anxiety, from which I had also suffered all my life. Although I am of an age to retire, I tend to just not think about it. So I am getting older but still at work. I have no plan for life after work. This job is a vocation for me, not just an occupation. It's a calling. Once you find your calling to be a therapist, why would you ever leave?

I am attached to my image of being a professional licensed therapist. It gives me a belief in my worth to others. I feel I would lose that by retiring and that I would have to make up for that loss of what I will call "usefulness." My value is being linked to being useful. It is just so ingrained in me from my entire life that I should be hardworking (useful with every moment of my day) and efficient. That makes the idea of retirement feel really foreign to me and hard to do. I am old enough to retire, but far from willing to make this change.

I really struggled with this issue for years, whether to retire or not. I loved my work and was not ready to leave it, but I agreed to my husband's fervent desire for us both to retire. What he didn't understand was that my professional identity gave me a sense of purpose, competency, and meaning. Now my world revolves around being with him, and when we go sailing, my new identity is "first mate" on an ocean-going sailboat for several months a year. It has none of the purpose and value that I got from my work, and it is such a contrast with my work values of helping others. I feel guilty for being prosperous enough to retire like this when so many can't afford the basics, and for leaving my clients just to seek retirement and pleasure with my husband.

I so loved being in charge of a team. I didn't know about managing or leading until I became the deputy director of clinical training in my agency. I didn't ever want to leave, but one day, a colleague—a board member—began to talk with me about succession planning for my position. I was seventy and heartbroken but understood that younger and deserving therapists were waiting in the wings. I took a year to step down, but I still felt rushed. I wasn't really ready to retire, but my agency wanted me out. So I left. I still miss it. I miss my role, my office, my team, and the structure it gave to my days and weeks. I haven't found anything to replace it yet. I feel angry, like it wasn't fair, even though I understand why it had to happen. No one looks to me these days for guidance or instruction or planning. I have little use for all the leadership skills I worked so hard to acquire.

For some at the precontemplation stage, the answer to the stay or go dilemma is to minimize their work: reduce their caseload or working hours and let things dwindle down. If they work for an organization, they try to cut back to part-time, then quarter-time. It's hard for them to decide to retire, to make a clean break and just walk away.

Therapists we hear from at this stage often express uncertainty. They wonder how long they can remain in limbo, caught between the decision of whether to stay or go. There's also concern about the potential consequences—sometimes unforeseen—if they don't begin to at least consider, let alone plan for, retirement.

> The truth is that if I did not have this very small practice, I don't know who I would be. As long as I can listen, I want to be a working therapist. I love hearing stories. Describing myself as a grandma, which is definitely an important part of my life outside of work, doesn't seem to say all that I am. But I guess I might be inclined to think about retirement if I can find a role that uses my skills, like being an elder in the community. That sounds good to me. Finding small ways to contribute meaningfully could be the new description of my life.

> Last night I was thinking about my age, seventy-six, and the fact that I have no vision for my life outside of work. I began to journal and to think about how long I can keep going and how long I even want to keep going. I cried a little, because this change of leaving my career will be hard for me. But I also started to think about the need to find a bright light for my remaining years. I could live to be one-hundred, and I want to make sure I have no regrets.

> I think I am in denial, because I keep pretending at sixty-eight that I am not aging and not slowing down (even though my body says differently). I have some chronic health problems that are not going to go away. I came to your webinar hoping for a silver bullet, an easy way out of this fantasy of thinking I can keep working forever, but alas, there isn't one. I am going to have to take the hard step of facing reality and begin making some decisions about when and how I will retire. I have time, but I realize that if I don't make these choices, circumstances will make them for me.

Your Turn

Did any of these voices speak to you personally? How would you respond if you were in conversation with these therapists? Would you empathize? Disagree? Offer suggestions? Share your own experience? Choose whatever voices spoke to you and respond here:

Contemplation: "Saying goodbye to client after client was hard and unremitting."

At our retirement workshops, the mood shifts noticeably when we introduce the second stage of readiness: *Contemplation: The Therapeutic Conversation* (chapters 4–6). This stage can be particularly challenging, as it forces therapists to confront the reality of ending their relationships with clients, associates, interns, colleagues, and peers. It's a stage that involves saying goodbye to those who rely on us and whom we deeply impact. As we discuss the contemplation stage, participants transition from passive listeners to active speakers. They raise their hands, eager to share, and the conversation often becomes both emotional and intense.

Some therapists are reluctant to let this stage of contemplation come to a resolution, instead remaining stuck in the uncertainty of indecision. Others may want to retire but feel unsure about how to close their practices without disrupting ongoing treatment. As therapists, we don't close cases lightly, recognizing that for many clients, we are a lifeline—something not easily replaced.

Consider these comments about the very real complexity of initiating a forced ending in therapy, shared by those who have navigated this stage. As therapists reflect on the attachment their clients have to them and to the therapy sessions, they also recognize their own emotional attachment to the work and the relationships they've built.

> I was okay about retiring in terms of the steps and actions to take, and I understood the logistics. But my emotions were a totally different thing. Having to say goodbye to twenty plus clients a week was grueling. The emotional aspect of saying goodbye to client after client was hard and unremitting. Session after session, I never knew what to expect. Many said that I had changed their lives, and they were probably right. Others were upset and angry with me and accused me of not caring about them. Post-sessions, I often cried and worried and wrote my final notes, hoping that they would be okay but wondering if I would. It took a full year to close things down.

> The biggest challenge for me was making sure I could financially afford to retire. But the second biggest challenge was having to separate completely from people I cared about and would never see again or even know how they were doing. I knew this was how it worked for a therapist—you say goodbye and there is no coming back—but man, was it hard to do this.

> My connection with clients was so important to me. It was such a privilege to get to know people and be with them through their struggles. When people ask me if I miss my work, that's what I say. I mourned when I gave up my practice. In your workshop, you explained attachment styles in ending, both in clients and in the therapist. This approach finally showed me why it was so hard for me to end with some of them. My own grief is related to my family-of-origin history. My parents died when I was young and I didn't get to say goodbye. Ending with clients, even though it was my choice, stirred a lot of that trauma up for me again.

> I spent a year reading through client files after I retired, reviewing the work and enjoying some of the breakthrough moments with clients as well as feeling sad for others who did not do so well. I often wonder how some of those clients are doing. I know some of us say that our clients were like family, but really, I saw my clients much more often than I saw my extended family. No one in my family really talks to each other, so my clients did feel like a kind of family experience for me. No wonder I am still thinking about cases even two years post-retirement.

In this second stage of readiness, the process of leaving can take an emotional and psychological toll on the therapist. Therapist reactivity or countertransference may surface as therapists try to monitor their own feelings. Some therapists feel pressured and guilty, especially if they need to stop sooner than they thought based on their own illness or family demands. Others may have the luxury of time, but even having time to plan does not resolve all the feelings that are present. Therapists often tell us that their own history or feelings about endings in general may start to appear to them in fantasies, dreams, or reflections about mortality, abandonment, or loneliness.

> Each month as I got closer to my retirement announcement to clients, I began to question everything about my work: my competence, my value, if I had made a difference. I wondered about the lack of real measures for results in our profession and what I could honestly say about the work I do. I know that this was part of my grieving process, but at the time it felt very real, and I was quite upset and uncertain about my career. I had no one to talk to about this; none of my close colleagues were retiring. It was a very hard time for me, having so little support.

> I needed to leave my small practice, filled with some very long-term clients, to relocate and take care of my mother, whose health was failing. She lived in Florida. I guess I was pretty ready to stop working—maybe burned out after the pandemic—because I just couldn't wait to go. The idea of only taking care of one other person instead of a dozen was so appealing. When clients wanted to review their time with me and deal with their sadness, a part of me was impatient. I felt like, enough already. Why drag this out? Let's get it done. I know this was my stuff, but it made it hard to stay empathic about what they were going through and to give them my full empathy. I just kept dreaming of being on the beach with a book.

During this time of making an announcement and saying goodbye, I began to dream about my own death. I saw myself swimming in a lake and slowly sinking to the bottom. It was a recurring dream and so intensely upsetting that I went back into therapy to explore it. In the dream, I was very fearful of sinking down to the bottom. Interpreting the dream, I understood that this profession—becoming a therapist—raised me up beyond all my expectations of who or what I could be. My career was one of advancement. I went beyond anyone in my family in terms of degree, income, and business ownership. I made money and supported myself, published a book, and gave talks. I used this dream interpretation to begin to actively plan for what would come next so that I wouldn't feel lost or face a huge letdown when I finally retired. I made sure I had something good and uplifting to look forward to.

Your Turn

Did any of these voices speak to you personally? How would you respond if you were in conversation with these therapists? Would you empathize? Disagree? Offer suggestions? Share your own experience? Choose whatever voices spoke to you and respond here:

Preparation: "I longed for a roadmap to help guide me out of the forest that was my practice."

We know that part of retirement planning is purely pragmatic. In the third stage of the Readiness for Retirement Model, *Preparation: The Logistics of Letting Go* (chapters 7–9), much of the conversation focuses on logistics: What should I do? What steps do I need to take? In our interviews, some therapists spoke about using extensive to-do lists during the preparation stage, while others admitted to feeling unsure if they were taking the right steps. Depending on the situation and their level of readiness to retire, it seemed that each step forward stirred either excitement or anxiety.

I knew I was ready to retire from a solo practice but had no idea what to do first or even second. It felt like I was on a journey, but through a dense wood, and I couldn't get my bearings. Really, there was no one I knew who was in my situation who could help. I longed for a roadmap to help guide me out of the forest that was my practice. I did the best I could, but looking back, I think I ended some cases too abruptly. I am not sure that I communicated well with clients, and I was so overwhelmed with the work of exiting from insurance rolls and making sure that I was in compliance with all my billing and statements that I just felt nervous and anxious. The day I closed the office door and turned out the lights was particularly hard; it felt like such a quiet ending. No one there to walk me out or hold my hand—it was just me.

I had what I thought was a good plan. I would phase out by not taking clients that I knew would require longer-term work and with whom the therapeutic relationship would be critical, so for two years before I planned to retire, I declined taking new clients like that, such as trauma survivors. Then I did not take any new clients at all other than very short-term people for a year. I was going to phase out by attrition. But surprise, then COVID hit and I had a rash of returning clients by virtual therapy, so I ended up working very long hours instead of the relaxed attrition I planned. I had to wait until that wave slowed, so I worked another year. Finally, after that, I took the leap and quit altogether.

I own a group practice and no longer work with clients. Instead, I do a lot of networking, dealing with day-to-day problems, and overseeing insurance issues, and then I have an open door for supervision and mentoring with the therapists who work with me. Most are independent contractors, and I am spending a lot of time trying to make sure that this practice goes on without me. I don't want to just shut this down. This is a job and a half, trying to figure out how I can leave but have the practice live on. I will really miss some of these other therapists. I am not sure how much we will see each other when I retire, but right now we see each other almost every day, and I look forward to the collegiality.

Two years before I left my practice, I met with a lawyer, my accountant, and a clinical supervisor to figure out what steps to take to end my work. It was a very long list, but I did my best to attend to everything. I tried to refer clients to colleagues, but some decided to quit and many ended up leaving first, before me. I hope I did this right; there was really no manual or policy to follow. One thing that helped a lot was that I joined a gym, and anytime I felt anxious, I would go work out. I think I wanted to be strong inside and out so that the leaving process would not deplete me.

Because I had a gradually reduced client load at my agency over several years, I felt like I had the best of both worlds. I was still engaged with a few clients, and I could take part in staff meetings as I wanted and make some money on the side to pay for art supplies and workshops. I had a good relationship with the director of the agency, who wanted me to work as much or as little as I wished. It was a combination of walking toward the future as well as away from the past.

We listened as therapists decided when and how to take the next large or small steps. We heard about the need for resources and a longing for more support from colleagues, to feel safer and more secure by knowing that their process was one that was understood and established. We appreciated the hard work of ending and the desire to stay resilient as they defined a timeline for closing large and small practices.

When I ended my work, I felt like I could write a manual. I had a nonprofit clinic I founded with interns and employees working with me. I made my decision to close up shop because I couldn't find a buyer for the clinic. Then there was so much I had to figure out to do. I had to put my clinical hat on the shelf and stop my work with clients so that I could wear my business hat for a year. It was tough to make provisions for all the clients and make sure that my interns and therapist-employees had sufficient notice to end, transfer, or refer out their caseloads. I felt depressed and anxious for much of that year. No one was very happy with the decisions I made, but I did the best I could, and frankly, I think I ended it with integrity.

Your Turn

Did any of these voices speak to you personally? How would you respond if you were in conversation with these therapists? Would you empathize? Disagree? Offer suggestions? Share your own experience? Choose whatever voices spoke to you and respond here:

Action: "Being retired brings your age—and how you are aging—front and center."

The final stage of the Readiness for Retirement Model is *Action: A New Beginning* (chapters 10–12). At the action stage, we hear therapists beginning to prepare themselves emotionally, psychologically, and practically to think ahead. They think about what they are walking toward in retirement, not just what they are walking away from.

> I am a little surprised that I feel like I am still participating in life and bringing some value to the world, given my reduced level of structured activity. It's been hard to create a new balance between endeavor and ease. Being retired brings your age—and how you are aging—front and center. I am trying not to focus on how much time I might have left and enjoy the moment I'm in. It's a challenge, but I'm working on it, and some days I can say I am quite content to be retired.

> What is great about being retired is the ease with which I can go about my life. I rarely feel rushed anymore. The paradox is as I get older, I find myself wanting to just be at home, in a routine, and doing simple things. Now, when I am asked or am introduced to people, I no longer refer to myself as a social worker, but rather: retired. The overriding thought is that I have more time behind me than in front of me.

> Was I walking away in retirement or walking toward? I didn't feel like I was walking away, but rather that my contribution was finished. I always felt some level of stress and worry about my practice, and it was a real burden. I am glad not to carry that anymore. In the process, the main thing I learned about myself is how important feelings of efficacy and relevance are to me.

Making a big change in life requires flexibility and resilience. Not every therapist we talk with is happy about retirement, and we listen to understand why this might be. Some have found a retirement identity easy to assume, while others have fallen into old patterns that don't transfer well into a retired lifestyle.

> Now in retirement, I spend an exorbitant amount of time taking care of details that either didn't get taken care of when I worked or someone else took care of them for me. For example, I was reading a book in my living room and heard birds chirping in my fireplace. There was a nest of baby birds in my fireplace! I had forgotten to get a cap for my chimney, which had been suggested to me the last time I had the chimney cleaned. Working at least forty-five hours a week, who remembers to get a cap for the chimney? The bird's nest reminded me that I had neglected far too many details at home.

> You know, I think I left my practice as a school counselor because I was angry: angry with the lack of support for mental health providers from the education bureaucrats, angry at the rate of pay school counselors received, and when I started a part-time practice, I was angry about the issues trying to be a provider for insurance companies. It felt like a cycle of low status and low pay, despite the important work that therapists do. So I quit everything. I was sixty; it seemed fair to retire, and I could afford it financially. But now I miss it. I don't want to repeat my pattern by volunteering and feeling resentful for a lot of work, and again having low status and pay. I quit without a plan and it felt like I was forced to leave due to my frustrations, but I am at a loss right now. I don't know what I left for, to be honest.

> I was a very hard worker in my career; I often saw up to forty clients a week, which is more than full time for most therapists. So no surprise, I need to keep very busy in retirement. I find projects and have probably taken on way too much. I got on two boards of volunteer organizations, manage the calendar for my local ladies table tennis team, and became the unofficial travel agent when a small group of friends decided to take a cruise. I think I need to slow down and find a new way of being so that I am not just recreating my work life in retirement.

In our workshops, we take time to focus on the concept of legacy for a therapist. What can you take with you from the arc of your career, and how it will serve you in the future? In this stage, we hear some fear, but also some excitement. We hear some sadness or grief about what is left behind, but also a new self-assurance and purpose as therapists think ahead.

I have never dreamt of retirement myself. I love my work. But my family wants me to retire, travel, and be with them, and I am really thinking about how nice it might be to refocus on other goals. I still want a life that includes purpose and meaning, so I will do something with my time—find volunteer opportunities, I guess. But this is a chance to find a new side of life and maybe a new side of myself. I want to find what else I can love.

I have learned a lot about the value of being present as I have walked through dying with two friends in the last year. Productivity does not save lives or communicate to others how I value them. Mortality is clearly on my horizon, given my age. Awareness of that has me planning to travel and visiting with friends while I still have health. I have some clear priorities of what I need and want more of at this time, and it is not being practical or even useful to others. My goals are being with people I care about and doing all I can to enjoy them.

I love to travel. I love to have fun. Work got in the way of having fun. Mom said, "You have to plan how to be older when you are young." I remembered that and created a life that was fun. Work was not everything—just moving to the next opportunity.

After I retire, which will happen in the next year, I am taking steps so that I will continue to be a helper but on a broader level. I am interested in things like climate change, politics, and other macro issues. I want to focus on a wider perspective of the global culture and world community. I see this direction as a possibility of a new life's work for me—a third act.

Your Turn

Did any of these voices speak to you personally? How would you respond if you were in conversation with these therapists? Would you empathize? Disagree? Offer suggestions? Share your own experience? Choose whatever voices spoke to you and respond here:

Letting Go of the Work You Love

We are now at the final stage of our journey together. We hope this workbook has helped you gain a deeper understanding of the unique process of retirement and the complexities of letting go of the work we all love. As we see it, the Readiness for Retirement Model is more evolution than revolution; it outlines a natural process of change that you can navigate at your own pace, focusing on the stages that require more time and revisiting sections when you need additional encouragement or preparation. The stages follow each other in an intuitively progressive manner, and we encourage you to move through them, finding your own insightful and deliberate path.

Throughout this journey, we've spoken to you in professional terms, drawing from a theoretical framework of change that blends with our direct experience as therapists. We recognize that the process of retirement for therapists is complex. We've addressed not just the "how to," but also the "how to be," offering what we believe you need to not only to retire, but retire well.

Embracing the final steps of a career can bring anxiety—the future is never certain—but preparation can ease that uncertainty. We know this time can be one of rich reward, affirming all you've tried to share with your clients throughout your career: That life, if you are willing to engage, never stops helping you grow. As your abilities change and develop during your retirement years, we hope you find opportunities for contentment and satisfaction in a career well done and a life well-lived.

Final Words

I (Margaret) came out of retirement to write a workbook about retiring. In doing so, noting what I had done well as I retired and what I skipped in the preparation stage let me review my own process. I celebrated what had worked and noted some gaps in my own preparation that helped me shape the elements we suggested here. Writing my other books had always had an element of demand to fit them around the "real work" of psychotherapy. Being retired, I finally had time to just write. Doing a project I loved, utilizing my experience and my skills, was fun, and time to focus and complete it without a rush was a treat. I had the great joy of working with Lynn, a thinker, a writer, and an editor of great talent. This workbook is more than twice as good because of our collaboration than it would have been preparing it alone.

I (Lynn) had the unique opportunity to prepare for retirement through writing, researching, and collaborating with Margaret over the past five years. We had time to think deeply about the process—conducting focus groups, doing interviews, and reading everything we could. As this book took shape, it began to reshape me as well. Unlike my other writing, this project forced me to slow down, go inward, and wrestle with my own thoughts and beliefs about bringing my career to a peaceful and satisfying close.

I'm not ready to retire yet, but I now have a clear sense of what the experience will likely hold for me, how to prepare and plan, and how to approach this stage of life with honesty and openness, without fear. I also had the privilege of working closely with Margaret, who is brilliant and generous. I'm so grateful she came out of retirement to write with me. Our collaboration was a true joy—one filled with teamwork and free from ego—where we were both able to enjoy both the journey *and* the destination.

Bibliography

For your convenience, exercises from this book are available for download at www.pesipubs.com/lettinggo.

Barnett, J. E., & Coffman, C. (2015, July 5) *Termination and abandonment.* Society for the Advancement of Psychotherapy. https://societyforpsychotherapy.org/termination-and-abandonment-a-proactive-approach-to-ethical-practice

Barnett, J. E., Knapp, S., Handelsman, M. M., & Kastenberg, J. E. (2024). Key issues and recommendations for ethical and effective endings in psychotherapy. *Professional Psychology: Research and Practice*, *55*(2), 129–139. https://doi.org/10.1037/pro0000566

Blasco-Belled, A., & Alsinet, C. (2022). The architecture of psychological well-being: A network analysis study of the Ryff Psychological Well-Being Scale. *Scandinavian Journal of Psychology*, *63*(3), 199–207. https://doi.org/10.1111/sjop.12795

Brooks, A. C. (2024, July 4). *Declare your independence—from misery.* The Atlantic. https://www.theatlantic.com/ideas/archive/2024/07/declaration-independence-misery-happiness/678860

Buettner, D. (2017). *The blue zones of happiness: Lessons from the world's happiest people*. National Geographic.

Covey, S. R. (1989). *The 7 habits of highly effective people*. Free Press.

Duncan, B. L., Miller, S. D., Wampold, B. E., & Hubble, M. A. (Eds.) (2010). *The heart and soul of change: delivering what works in therapy* (2nd ed.). American Psychological Association.

Erikson, E. (1994). *Identity and the life cycle* (Reissue ed.). W.W. Norton.

Faverio, M. (2022, January 13). *Share of those 65 and older who are tech users has grown in the past decade*. Pew Research Center. https://www.pewresearch.org/short-reads/2022/01/13/share-of-those-65-and-older-who-are-tech-users-has-grown-in-the-past-decade

Freire, B. (2017). *Retirement, a new opportunity*. LID Editorial Empresarial, S.L.

Freire, B., & Margolies, R. (2024, April 7). *Retirement: Challenges and opportunities* [Virtual conference presentation]. Center for the Study of Aging and Clinical Applications.

Gelles-Watnick, R. (2024). *Americans' use of mobile technology and home broadband.* Pew Research Center. https://www.pewresearch.org/internet/2024/01/31/americans-use-of-mobile-technology-and-home-broadband

Godin, S. (2018) *This is marketing*. Portfolio Publishing.

Greer, N. (2023). *The seven traits of change-readiness.* University of North Carolina at Charlotte. https://continuinged.charlotte.edu/articles/hr/change-readiness

Griffin, M. (2010, March/April). Closing a psychotherapy practice: Further considerations. *The Therapist.* California Association of Marriage and Family Therapists. https://www.camft.org/Portals/0/PDFs/articles/closing_psychotherapy_practice.pdf?ver=2019-05-27-122835-790

Grodzki, L. (2015). *Building your ideal private practice* (2nd ed.). W. W. Norton.

Grodzki, L., & Wehrenberg, M. (2024, January/February). *Saying goodbye to work you love.* Psychotherapy Networker. https://www.psychotherapynetworker.org/article/saying-goodbye-to-work-you-love

Groshong, L. (2023, September 29). *Practice endings, planned and unplanned* [Webinar]. Clinical Social Work Association. https://www.clinicalsocialworkassociation.org/event-5377572

Heys, E. (2024, June 26). *Cultural evolution: Measuring differences in generational values.* Berkeley Institute for Young Americans. https://youngamericans.berkeley.edu/2024/06/cultural-evolution-measuring-differences-in-generational-values

Hitchcott, P. K., Fastame, M. C., & Penna, M. P. (2018). More to Blue Zones than long life: Positive psychological characteristics. *Health, Risk, and Society*, *20*(3–4), 163–181. https://doi.org/10.1080/13698575.2018.1496233

Ingram, J., Hand, C. J., & Maciejewski, G. (2021). Social isolation during COVID-19 lockdown impairs cognitive function. *Applied Cognitive Psychology*, *35*(4), 935–947. https://doi.org/10.1002/acp.3821

International Center for Clinical Excellence. (2102). *What works in therapy: A primer.* Manual 1: ICCE Manuals on Feedback-Informed Treatment (FIT). https://fit-elearning.myoutcomes.com/Content/docs/Manual_1.pdf

Jung, C. G. (1923). *Psychological types: Or the psychology of individuation.* Harcourt, Brace, and Company.

Jung, C. G. (1972). *Collected Works of C. G. Jung, Volume 8: The structure and dynamics of the psyche* (2nd ed.). Princeton University Press.

Keshishian, A. (Director). (1991). *Truth or dare.* [Film]. Boy Toy, Inc.; Propaganda Films.

Kim, E. S., Strecher, V. J., & Ryff, C. D. (2014). Purpose in life and use of preventive health care services. *Proceedings of the National Academy of Sciences of the United States*, *111*(46), 16331–16336. https://doi.org/10.1073/pnas.1414826111

Kinder, George. (1999). *The seven stages of money maturity: Understanding the spirit and value of money in your life.* Delacorte Press.

Koenig, H. G. (2006). Religion, spirituality and aging. *Aging & Mental Health*, *10*(1), 1–3. https://doi.org/10.1080/13607860500308132

Krause, N. (2004). Stressors arising in highly valued roles, meaning in life, and the physical health status of older adults. *The Journals of Gerontology Series B: Psychological Sciences and Social Sciences*, *59*(5), S287–S297. https://doi.org/10.1093/geronb/59.5.s287

Landi, H. (2022, November 1). *More than 300k healthcare providers dropped out of the workforce in 2021, report finds.* Fierce Healthcare. https://www.fiercehealthcare.com/providers/more-300k-healthcare-providers-dropped-out-workforce-2021-report-finds

Maslow, A. H. (1943). A theory of human motivation. *Psychological Review*, *50*(4), 370–396. https://doi.org/10.1037/h0054346

Manzi, C., Paderi, F., & Benet-Martinez, V. (2024). Multiple social identities and well-being: Insights from a person-centred approach. *British Journal of Social Psychology*, *63*(2), 792–810. https://doi.org/10.1111/bjso.12704

Miller, R. (2024). TheraClosure. https://www.theraclosure.com

Miscenko, D., & Day, D. V. (2016). Identity and identification at work. *Organizational Psychology Review*, *6*(3), 215–247. https://doi.org/10.1177/2041386615584009

Mountain Dreamer, Oriah. (2006) *The invitation*. (Reprint ed.). HarperOne.

National Association of Social Workers Center for Workforce Studies (2012, February) *Retiring? Tips for closing your private practice.* https://www.naswma.org/page/486

National Endowment for Financial Education. (2021, November 18). *2 in 5 Americans admit to financial infidelity against their partner.* NEFE. https://www.nefe.org/news/2021/11/2-in-5-americans-admit-to-financial-infidelity-against-their-partner.aspx

Naparstek, B. (1995). *Staying well with guided imagery*. Warner Books.

Neufeld, D. (2020, September 17). *Visualizing the hierarchy of financial needs.* Advisor Channel. https://advisor.visualcapitalist.com/hierarchy-of-financial-needs

Olsen, R. B., Olsen, J., Gunner-Svensson, F., & Waldstrøm, B. (1991). Social networks and longevity. A 14 year follow-up study among elderly in Denmark. *Social Science and Medicine*, *33*(10), 1189–1195. https://doi.org/10.1016/0277-9536(91)90235-5

Power, A. (2015). *Forced endings in psychotherapy and psychoanalysis: Attachment and loss in retirement*. Routledge.

Prochaska, J. O., & DiClemente, C. C. (1983). Stages and processes of self-change of smoking: Toward an integrative model of change. *Journal of Consulting and Clinical Psychology*, *51*(3), 390–395. https://doi.org/10.1037/0022-006X.51.3.390

Prochaska, J. O., & Prochaska, J. M. (1999). Why don't continents move? Why don't people change? *Journal of Psychotherapy Integration*, *9*(1), 83–102. https://doi.org/10.1023/A:1023210911909

reddit_rabbit507. (2024). *I've been in practice for 35 years as a psychologist. No retirement plans in sight for me.* [Comment on the online forum post *How long after closing practice can you end malpractice insurance?*] Reddit. https://www.reddit.com/r/therapists/comments/1bw1jo8/how_long_after_closing_practice_can_you_end

Rosenzweig, S. (1936). Some implicit common factors in diverse methods of psychotherapy. *American Journal of Orthopsychiatry*, *6*(3), 412–415. https://doi.org/10.1111/j.1939-0025.1936.tb05248.x

Ryff, C. D., & Keyes, C. L. M. (1995). The structure of psychological well-being revisited. *Journal of Personality and Social Psychology*, *69*(4), 719–727. https://doi.org/10.1037//0022-3514.69.4.719

Shmotkin, D., Blumstein, T., & Modan, B. (2003). Beyond keeping active: Concomitants of being a volunteer in old-old age. *Psychology and Aging*, *18*(3), 602–607. https://doi.org/10.1037/0882-7974.18.3.602

Shmotkin, D., & Shrira, A. (2012). On the distinction between subjective well-being and meaning in life: Regulatory versus reconstructive functions in the face of a hostile world. In P. T. P. (Ed.), *The human quest for meaning: Theories, research, and applications* (2nd ed., pp. 143–163). Routledge.

Siegel, B. (1999). *Love, medicine and miracles*. Random House.

Siracusa, F., Weber, J., Will, J., Coiro, K., Bates, K., Klein, J., Olsen, E. C., Urman, J. S., Renna, N., & Lieber, J. (Executive Producers). (2024–present). *Matlock* [TV series]. Sutton Street Productions; Cloud Nine Productions; CBS Studios.

Smith, A. (2013, June 5). *Smartphone ownership 2013.* Pew Research Center. https://www.pewresearch.org/internet/2013/06/05/smartphone-ownership-2013

Stein, M. (2019). *Map of the soul – Persona: Our many faces.* Chiron Publications.

Taylor, S. E., & Brown, J. D. (1988). Illusion and well-being: A social psychological perspective on mental health. *Psychological Bulletin, 103*(2), 193–210. https://doi.org/10.1037/0033-2909.103.2.193

Vaillant, G. E. (2003). *Aging well: Surprising guideposts to a happier life from the landmark study of adult development* (Reprint ed.). Little, Brown Spark.

Walsch, N. D. (1996). *Conversations with God: An uncommon dialogue* (Book 1). G. P. Putnam's Sons.

Wehrenberg, M. (2008). *The 10 best-ever anxiety management techniques: Understanding how your brain makes you anxious and what you can do to change it.* W. W. Norton.

Whitman, W. (2023). *Leaves of grass.* SeaWolf Press. (Original published in 1892).

Winnicott, D. W. (1991). *Playing and reality.* Psychology Press.

About the Authors

Lynn Grodzki, LCSW, is a psychotherapist and Master Certified Coach (MCC) who has been in private practice since 1990. A pioneer in the field of practice development, she is the author of six books, including *Building Your Ideal Private Practice* and *Therapy with a Coaching Edge*. Her articles have appeared in publications such as the *Psychotherapy Networker* magazine and *Social Work Today*. She is a popular presenter at conferences and offers workshops and webinars to continuing education providers. She can be reached at her website: privatepracticesuccess.com.

Margaret Wehrenberg, PsyD, is a clinical psychologist with fifty years of experience in the mental health field. She's the author of thirteen books, including the bestselling *10 Best-Ever Anxiety Management Techniques*. Margaret has contributed numerous articles to the *Psychotherapy Networker* magazine and has blogged for *Psychology Today*. In addition to her private psychotherapy practice, she trained mental health professionals across the United States and internationally over the past thirty years for many continuing education providers. She is currently enjoying an active and happy retirement.